# SPOTTING BIRDS

# SPOTTING BIRDS

## A POCKET GUIDE TO BIRD WATCHING

by Jaroslav Spirhanzl Duriš
and Edmund Burke

Illustrated by Jan Solovjev

**HAMLYN**

Designed and produced by Artia for
The Hamlyn Publishing Group Ltd
London — New York — Sydney — Toronto
Astronaut House, Feltham, Middlesex, England
© Jaroslav Spirhanzl Duriš 1961, Illustrations © Jan Solovjev 1961
English text © Paul Hamlyn Ltd 1964
Original text translated by Hedda Veselá-Stránská
First Published 1964
Revised edition 1967
Reprinted 1968, 1969, 1970, 1971, 1972, 1973, 1974, 1975

ISBN 0 600 03614 6

Printed in Czechoslovakia by PZ Bratislava
3/02/03/51

# INTRODUCTION

Have you ever stopped to think just how important birds are to us? We all know something about birds, whether we live in the city or in the country, but most of us never really stop to think about them. Sitting here now, writing this, there have been seven different birds outside the window — Great Tits, Blue Tits, Song Thrushes, Jackdaws, House Sparrows, Tree Sparrows and a Wren. Many of you would see as many different kinds, if you looked carefully. You're probably asking right now, just how birds are important, what they really have to do with us. They're pretty, yes, many of them and their voices may be beautiful; they can be interesting and fun to watch — but why are they important? The answer lies in the fact that experts have judged that if all our birds suddenly left or died, man himself would cease to exist within a year.

Strange to think, isn't it, that the little sparrow taking crumbs in the street, and the flock of starlings roosting across the field control our very lives. For if all the birds were to disappear the insects of the world would multiply so rapidly there'd be nothing left for us. If you're thinking that we have developed chemical sprays and insecticides that would kill the insects, remember that insects in turn have developed immunity to those same sprays. In spite of all that science and chemistry have done for us we still need the birds, need them desperately.

The farmer's work would be a great deal harder if we had no birds, even forgetting the insects. Many of our common birds live almost entirely on weed seeds, so that with their help our crops are cleaner, our pastures give better grazing. Of course it isn't always possible for these seed eaters to tell the difference between weed seeds and seeds we might want for ourselves but they do a pretty good job and must be forgiven for a few errors.

Birds, and by that we mean all of them, from the humming bird to the Andean condor, are vitally important in preserving the balance of nature. Every living thing plays a part in that great pattern of existence and when we tamper with it by removing or destroying one of those parts, no one knows what the final result will be.

A few years ago farmers complained bitterly about the havoc which rabbits created in their fields and pastures. Then myxomatosis, a disease which came first from Brazil, was introduced and practically wiped out all our rabbits. The results of that epidemic are still not all known and we may not know them for many more years. As far as the farmers are concerned, many of them now feel that most of the damage wasn't done by rabbits after all but by wood pigeons. But it is the side effects which are still puzzling us, and are still making themselves felt. Foxes formerly ate many rabbits, which formed the basis of their diet. With no natural prey available foxes have raided poultry houses more than ever before, and even attacked cats and small dogs. Birds of prey such as hawks and falcons, which also ate many rabbits, have drifted elsewhere and as a result the other staples of their diet — rats, mice, voles and moles — have multiplied rapidly. Certain kinds of plants which rabbits themselves ate now grow unchecked, crowding out other more useful things. Perhaps in another ten years we will be able to say exactly what the disease has done, perhaps not, but we do know that it has seriously upset nature's own plan.

The extinction of any form of life can have far-reaching and long-range results, many of them harmful. When it actually happens we may feel that it is for the best but we can never be sure. At the very best, it would be a sad and dreary world without birds. So, because birds are lovely to look at, pleasant to hear, fascinating to study and invaluable allies of all mankind they are well worth watching. The hobby of bird watching is most rewarding, even though you may never follow it up to become an ornithologist. Becoming a bird watcher isn't hard for almost the entire world has a bird population and no matter where you are, there, too, will be birds. And if you stop to think, almost without doubt you've already done a bit of bird watching without realizing it. For instance, count up and see how many birds you can identify, right now. Probably a lot more than you have guessed, because birds are always with us, in the dead of winter or in high summer, and we learn about them without ever realizing it. Obviously the kind and number of birds we see depends on where we are — the birds of the forest are usually different from those of the field, and the ones we see around marshes are not the ones we find in towns; but all the same, there are always birds.

One thing which you need when you seriously begin to look for and at birds is a book on the subject. When you start you certainly don't want anything big, or even very technical. Rather, you want something you can slip into a pocket to have with you because you never know when you might see a bird you've not seen before and you'll want to identify it on the spot. You can very often remember the details to check on when you get home but it's always easier to look it up at that moment. Naturally, not every bird is pictured here — to show them would require a book many times the size of this one, but there are enough to give you a good start, and in addition there are some really rare ones, birds which normally live in Europe, reaching these islands only accidentally. You may never see one but at least if you do, you'll know what you've met.

Bird watching can start, not only in any place but at any time. We have more birds during the spring and summer months than at any other time of the year, but it is not necessarily true that it's better to begin at that time. Strange though it may sound, it is far easier to start when there aren't so many birds. If you do that, you have a chance to get to know the residents, the birds which are with us all year round, and then, as the migrants arrive, you can add them to your mental catalogue. Of course there are a few winter migrants too, birds which spend their winters with us, rather than the summers. They usually come from Arctic and sub-Arctic regions, and to them our winter is mild. There aren't many of them, though, and most of the birds you see in winter are those which spend their whole lives here.

One of the basic rules about bird watching, and about many other hobbies, is to begin slowly. It is far better to learn a few birds well; to know their colours, the way they fly, the colour of their eggs and the way they build their nests, than to try to learn a little bit about a lot of birds all at once.

Another of the first things you must learn about bird watching is that you do your best observing without being observed. Many of our birds — the Robin and the House Sparrow, for instance, are unafraid of man but many of the others are shy and mistrust us. When you're looking for that kind you must move softly and slowly, taking care that you see the bird and not the reverse. There's nothing worse than to see the flickering tail feathers of a shy stranger disappearing, after you've made a long and careful approach. Dress inconspicuously and wear soft shoes when possible. Don't stand out on the skyline where you stick out like a sore thumb, but move below the horizon, taking advantage of every bit of cover and never, never hurry. Learn to put your feet down carefully, without cracking every dead limb and twig in sight. Above all, learn to listen. Many times, in looking for birds whose plumage is dull and drab or well-camou-flaged by nature, your first clue will come from a call or a song. When you hear it, stop and wait patiently. The call will probably come again, and you can orient yourself to the sound. With a little practice you can learn to pinpoint a sound without difficulty and when you've done that it becomes easier to see the caller or singer as it perches against some mottled, blending background.

Field glasses or even opera glasses are a wonderful help when you're bird watching. Very often you'll find that while you can see the bird, you simply can't get close enough to make out all the fine points needed for a definite identification. There may be a hedge in the way or a little stream, although it is usually the fact that if you move any closer you'll frighten your 'quarry' away. Under those circumstances, glasses are the only answer because they take those vital last steps for you.

There are several ways in which you can learn more and more about birds. You can, for instance, learn something about a thrush and then 'spot' it immediately and without any question. The thrush family is a large one and if you know the Song Thrush well, you will know or at least guess, that the blackbird is also a thrush. When you've 'learned' the Blackbird, you'll begin to add other thrushes to your list — the Redwing, the Mistle Thrush, the Redstart and even our familiar friend the Robin. All of them have basic similarities called family characteristics, and once you've familiarized yourself with those characteristics you've gone more than halfway to identifying any member of the thrush family you've not seen before.

Another means of identification is by the call or song. Ducks, apart from having distinct likenesses to one another physically, have cries and calls which could belong to no other group; if you hear a 'quacking' it is bound to be a duck. With birds like warblers, which are shy and have for the most part dull plumage, sometimes the only real clue you have towards the identity of a certain bird is its song. Perhaps the only time when identification by voice can go wrong is when you meet birds which are imitators or mockers. A blackbird once learned to imitate a dog-whistle and seemed to delight in calling up the dogs around the kennel.

Nests and their construction, as well as their location, offer other excellent clues. Many people make the mistake of calling Swallows Martins and vice-versa. Even though they may not recognize the physical differences between the two birds, they build nests of an entirely different shape — the Swallow's open at the top like a big shallow cup; the Martin's rounded, with an entrance hole at one side. The eggs within the nest are also a great help in identification, but in a family such as the warblers it takes a real specialist to tell one from another. The shape, size and colouring of the eggs are often among the family characteristics. There's one point to remember though: if you do find a nest, don't disturb it, and don't take any of the eggs. We've long since collected all we need of each and every kind and it is far better to keep an eye on the nest from a distance than to rob or harm it.

Some of our birds fly in a way which makes them unmistakable. One of them is the Lapwing or Green Plover, whose flapping quickly identifies it. The silent flight of the owl is almost always a clue; their extremely soft feathers make them silent as they wing their way through the air. In contrast to the owls the swans beat through the air with a whistling sound you can never forget. Once you've heard a swan in flight you will always remember it.

Even the way birds walk will help you to know them. Tree Creepers walk up trees and fly down, while Nuthatches walk up or down but always cling closely to the trees, hugging the bark so to speak. And the Wagtails spurt about as they walk, moving in short darting lunges so that every time they stop they must balance themselves with their tails, which move up and down rapidly as the birds halt.

No method of 'identifying' birds is fool-proof and all these clues should be combined. And of course the best clue of all is plumage. Each bird has something distinctive about its colouring, something that marks it apart. The difference may be only small — the Rook looks almost exactly like the Carrion Crow, except that the Rook has bare nostrils — that is, there are small bare patches just above the beak on either side of its head. There are other ways by which you can tell the two birds apart — flight, nests, eggs and social habits (the Rook is a bird which likes company), but that one little difference in plumage will always give you your answer if everything else fails.

Naturally a Moorhen doesn't look like a Blackbird even though both seem black from a distance but that's where you bring all the other identification clues into use. Which bird walks this way, which has a certain call, which has peculiar feet, which has a distinctive beak? It can only be the combination that gives you the correct answer — but you can be helped a great deal by remembering what are called 'haunts', or sometimes 'habitats'. To be more precise, what sort of a bird can you expect to find in a certain place? Birds like to stay in special areas, places where they find nesting space and materials, and where their natural food is plentiful. These small areas are what we call their haunts and we can learn what type of bird to expect in each. There are as well, we all know, certain types of birds which roam far and wide, and have no real or fixed haunts save in nesting time, but they are usually the exception which proves the rule. In winter, for example, bands of Tits, Wrens, Nuthatches and other small residents flock together and roam all over the countryside in search of food. At other seasons these same birds are usually found only in their haunts. If we break down the different types of surroundings in which we might be watching for the bird residents we are in a much better position to identify what we see. One very simple list might include:

A) Areas where there are houses and other buildings but not necessarily cities.

1) On high spots and points — Blackbirds, Song Thrushes, Starlings and Jackdaws.

2) On garden fences or posts — Blue Tits, House Sparrows, Robins and Spotted Flycatchers.

B) Parks, commons and open land close to built-up areas: in small copses and along tree-lined avenues.

1) On high points — Starlings, Golden Orioles, Hawfinches, Blackbirds, Song Thrushes, Mistle Thrushes, Wood Warblers, Fieldfares, Redstarts, Chaffinches, Greenfinches and Goldfinches.

2) On tree trunks — Nuthatches and Tree Creepers.

3) In the undergrowth and bushes — Great Tits, Blue Tits, Marsh Tits, Coal Tits, Long-Tailed Tits, Tree Sparrows, Yellow Buntings, Red-Backed Shrikes, Blackcaps, Whitethroats, Lesser Whitethroats, Garden Warblers, Willow Warblers, Grasshopper Warblers and Nightingales.

C) In conifer forests, among the evergreen trees.

1) Within the forest itself — Blackbirds, Song Thrushes, Mistle Thrushes, Crossbills, Bullfinches, Siskins, Crested Tits, Coal Tits and Gold Crests.

2) In the undergrowth — Garden Warblers, Whitethroats, Robins, Great Tits, Blue Tits, Marsh Tits, Long-Tailed Tits, Wrens and Yellow Buntings.

3) In clearings within the forest and its edges —

Tree Pipits, Yellow Buntings, Stonechats, Whitethroats and Wrens.

D) On moors and waste lands.
1) Linnets, Greenfinches and Goldfinches, Yellow Buntings, Tree Sparrows, Stonechats, Sky Larks and Wood Larks, Meadow Pipits, Wheatears, Black Redstarts and Sand Martins.

E) In fields and meadows.
1) Sky Larks, Bramblings, Starlings, Yellow Buntings, Corn Buntings, Meadow Pipits, Blue-Headed Wagtails, Whinchats, Stonechats.

F) Near fast running fresh water.
1) Dippers, Wrens, Grey Wagtails and White Wagtails.

G) Near still water, among reed beds and in marshes.
1) Marsh Warblers, Reed Warblers, Sedge Warblers, Reed Buntings, Moorhens, Water Rails, Bitterns, Little Grebes, Great Crested Grebes and Mallards.

A listing like this isn't complete by any means, but it

will begin to give you an idea of how you can identify birds through knowing their haunts.

Although it may seem a little difficult and technical at first, one thing that is necessary in bird watching is to learn names of the various parts of the bird. Luckily, all birds are alike in this way and once you've learned the names they will serve you no matter where you're practising your hobby. If you read a description of a bird you've never seen — and of which there is no picture — you will be able to identify it when you actually do see it. All bird watchers use these same words for the same parts.

# THE PARTS OF A BIRD'S BODY

1. Forehead.
2. Crown.
3. Occipital region.
4. Nape.
5. Hind neck.
6. Mantle.
7. Back.
8. Rump.
9. Upper tail coverts.
10. Under tail coverts.
11. Belly.
12. Lower breast.

13. Upper breast.
14. Crop.
15. Front neck.
16. Throat.
17. Chin.
18. Bristles.
19. Lores.
20. Cheek.
21. Ear coverts.
22. Bend of wing.
23. Fore-edge of wing.
24. Tibia.

25. Scapula.
26. Tarsus.
27. Foot.
28. Toes.
29. Primaries.
30. Secondaries.
31. Scapulars.
32. Greater wing coverts.
33. Primary coverts.
34. Lesser wing coverts.
35. Bastard wings.
36. Tail feathers.

A bird is a wonderful thing, one of nature's most complex creations. Some - a very few - can be harmful or injurious to us but most of them are our friends, and good friends at that.

# THE PLATES

Plate 1

# THE LITTLE GREBE

*Podiceps ruficollis*

**EGGS:** Four to six laid between April and June, bluish white in colour, later stained reddish brown.

**NEST:** Usually a floating mass of water-weeds and sticks, sometimes at water's edge. When the parent birds leave the nest the eggs are covered with loose broken material from the nest itself.

**FOOD:** Small fish, fresh-water insects and crustaceans.

**HAUNTS:** Inland waters — lakes, ponds, mere and river estuaries. Occasionally driven into coastal waters by severe weather.

**GENERAL NOTES:** Also called the Dabchick, this is one of the smallest grebes, **Podicipitidae,** about ten inches in length. An accomplished diver, the Little Grebe is shy, with a soft calling note and a descending trill. Summer plumage is blackish with chestnut cheeks and throat. In winter the upper parts are lighter, with the underparts nearly white. In common with other members of the family new-hatched Little Grebes are precocious. As soon as they leave the egg they are water borr riding on their parents' backs.

Plate 1

*Plate 2*

# THE GREAT CRESTED GREBE

*Podiceps cristatus*

---

EGGS:      Three to six, off-white in colour. Laid between April and July.

NEST:      A large, tangled floating mass of waterweeds, reeds and other aquatic vegetation. When parent birds leave they cover the eggs with bits of the nest.

FOOD:      Small fish, tadpoles, crustaceans and insects. Obtained underwater by searching dives.

HAUNTS:    Inland waters — lakes, broads, canals and meres. Occasionally seen in brackish coastal waters.

GENERAL NOTES:      The largest of the grebes, the Great Crested, is easily distinguished by the ear-tufts on either side of its crest. Adult birds are usually silent but the young utter varying harsh cries. Like all grebes its toes are lobed rather than webbed. The distinctive neck frill is nearly black in spring, but is lost in autumn. Young birds lack the ear-tufts and frill, have grey-brown neck striping.

Plate 2

Plate 3

# THE CORMORANT

*Phalacrocorax carbo*

---

**EGGS:** Three to five of a dull, chalky white. Laid between April and May.

**NEST:** Communal nesting, normally on seacoasts. The nests are constructed roughly, of seaweed. Inland they are built with sticks.

**FOOD:** Fish and eels, obtained by deep swift diving.

**HAUNTS:** Coastal waters, including the tidal reaches of rivers. Occasionally found inland on larger bodies of water.

**GENERAL NOTES:** A large bird, the Cormorant shows plumage which is black, shading to dark brown, with a purple-green iridescence. The chin of the adult is white and in spring a white patch occurs across the thigh. Normally the birds are silent although they occasionally emit a harsh croak. In the Orient Cormorants are used by fishermen, neck rings being fitted to the birds which prevent their swallowing their catches. Here the bird is disliked because of its heavy depredations on sea fisheries.

Plate 3

Plate 4

# THE HERON

*Ardea cinerea*

---

EGGS:
: Three to five of a green-blue. Laid from February through March.

NEST:
: Large and clumsily built of sticks, usually in a tree but occasionally on cliff-tops. Herons nest communally in heronries, which may remain in use for centuries.

FOOD:
: Frogs, fish, eels, water insects, mice, voles and occasionally the young of aquatic birds.

HAUNTS:
: Almost universal distribution — coastal marshes, estuaries, rivers, lakes, meres and woodlands.

GENERAL NOTES:
: Blue-grey in colour with a whitish front. The beak is yellow and awl-shaped. The wings, which carry dark tips, move with a peculiar and unmistakable slow beat. The legs are elongated in flight with the long neck held in a pronounced S-curve. Adult birds may achieve a length of over three feet. Heronries in occupation are extremely noisy, the young birds being constantly hungry. Both parents feed the fledglings during the seven weeks in which they remain in the nest.

Plate 4

Plate 5

# THE BITTERN

*Botaurus stellaris*

---

EGGS:        From four to six, olive-green. Laid in early
             April to late May.

NEST:        Simple, built of grass or other marsh vegeta-
             tion on a platform of flattened reeds.

FOOD:        Frogs, worms, snails, crayfish and rarely mice.

HAUNTS:      Thick reed beds in fens and marshes. Breeds
             regularly in small numbers in the marshes of
             Norfolk and Suffolk and possibly a few other
             isolated places. Occurs also as a winter visitor.

GENERAL      One of the most handsome of our herons, the
NOTES:       Bittern carries a brown and buff plumage,
             barred with black. When disturbed these shy
             birds 'freeze' among the reeds, head held
             high. A variety of cries are recorded, the best-
             known being the booming of the male birds
             which can be heard for a distance of over a
             mile. The Bittern shares with the owl family
             an extremely soft plumage so that its flight is
             nearly soundless. The resident population of
             Great Britain having been nearly extermi-
             nated, the bird has now re-established itself
             in small numbers, largely due to protective
             measures.

Plate 5

Plate 6

# THE WHITE STORK

*Ciconia ciconia*

EGGS: Three to five, of a pure white. Laid from March through May.

NEST: A crude platform of sticks and branches, placed atop a convenient high point, often a chimney. Through continued use a nest may rise as high as five feet.

FOOD: Frogs, small mammals, reptiles, insects, sometimes small birds.

HAUNTS: Flatlands, particularly marshes, but the bird is highly adaptable.

GENERAL NOTES: A bird of good omen, the White Stork is widely protected in Europe. It is a large bird, some having been measured with a height of forty-four inches. It is pure white save for black wing coverts and quills. The beak, feet and legs are red. The White Stork nests as far north as Denmark but is only an irregular visitor to the British Isles. Formerly a stork's nest was said to bring good fortune to an entire town and the belief still prevails in many parts of the Continent.

Plate 6

Plate 7

# BEAN GOOSE

*Anser fabalis*

EGGS: Three to six; off-white, though may be stained. Laid in late May and June.

NEST: Scraped in the ground, near water; composed of grasses, mosses, dried leaves and down.

FOOD: Buds, leaves, grasses, cultivated grains, stubble.

HAUNTS: Lakes and rivers in the forested Arctic regions. A winter visitor to a few inland fresh-water areas of Britain.

GENERAL NOTES: The Bean Goose is similar to the more common Pink-Footed Goose, but is distinguished by its orange bill and feet and its larger size — about thirty-three inches. It breeds far to the north in Scandinavia and over to Siberia, but summers all over Europe except in Britain where it is limited to parts of Southern Scotland and Northern England. It arrives in Britain about October, remaining until March or April.

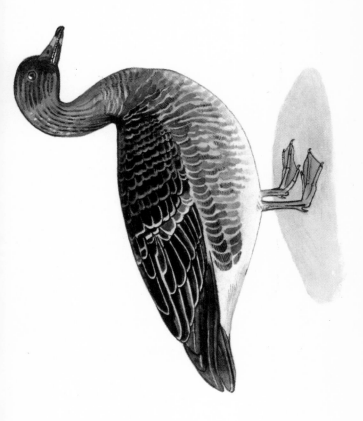

Plate 7

Plate 8

# THE MALLARD

*Anas platyrhynchos*

EGGS: From ten to fourteen, of an olive-white shade, laid normally in March.

NEST: Grass or any other convenient vegetation with a down lining, and located almost anywhere — field, woodland, marsh or even in low trees.

FOOD: Fish, insects, frogs, grain, fruit, snails, berries, practically omnivorous.

HAUNTS: During the summer, the immediate region around any type of fresh water. In winter months Mallards congregate along the sea shore.

GENERAL NOTES: A resident in Great Britain, the Mallard is widely known in both the Old World and the New. The drake's bottle green head and rufous markings are lost in the summer-summer moult, when he becomes nearly indistinguishable from the drabber, brown-mottled duck. The annual hatch of ducklings normally remains with the duck until late autumn.

Plate 8

Plate 9

# THE TEAL

*Anas crecca*

EGGS: Nine to twelve of a green or light buff shade. Laid usually between late April and early May.

NEST: Grasses and other vegetation with a down lining. Located in reed beds or woodlands adjacent to teal haunts.

FOOD: Crustaceans, small fish, insects, grain and aquatic plants.

HAUNTS: In summer, lakes, ponds and meres, moving to estuaries or coastal waters during winter.

GENERAL NOTES: One of our handsomest ducks, the tiny Teal is a British resident although our population is increased by migrants during the winter months. The rich chestnut head with its metallically shining green band marks the drake in his courtship plumage. After the summer moult the distinctive marks are lost and the drake looks much like the duck. The drake whistles softly but clearly, and the duck has a short harsh quack. The Teal is only about two-thirds as large as the more common Mallard.

Plate 9

Plate 10

# THE SPARROW HAWK

*Accipiter nisus*

EGGS: From four to six, off-white with reddish or brown blotching, usually confined to one end. Laid late, usually in May.

NEST: Roughly constructed of sticks, usually in densely wooded areas and built high in the trees.

FOOD: Small birds, up to and including partridge; has been known to take young chickens. Will also take mice, voles, frogs and large insects.

HAUNTS: Wood and meadow lands by preference but will come into inhabited areas in pursuit of prey. A bird or pair of birds will haunt an area for years, once established.

GENERAL NOTES: Fiercest of our native hawks, it may be identified by its rapid flight, the sudden drops on prey below. Hunts with outstretched talons, rakes hedgerows with great speed. Female two inches larger than the male.

Plate 10

Plate 11

# THE GOSHAWK

*Accipiter gentilis*

EGGS: From two to five, of a bluish white. Laid during May and June.

NEST: Crudely made of sticks and branches. Normally high in a tree and located close to the trunk. Nest is usually permanent and used year after year.

FOOD: Pigeons, rooks, crows, jackdaws, thrushes, starlings, domestic poultry, rabbits and even hares.

HAUNTS: Sparsely inhabited areas of Europe, showing a marked tendency to live in those areas which will supply it with adequate food.

GENERAL NOTES: The Goshawk is not a resident here, and is seen only occasionally. It resembles the Sparrow Hawk in almost every detail, save that it is about one-third larger and proportionately more destructive. Its habits are like those of its smaller cousin. Formerly widely used as a hunting hawk, it is still a favourite with falconers, when obtainable. One peculiarity of the Goshawk is the fact that it will not hunt in the immediate vicinity of the nest.

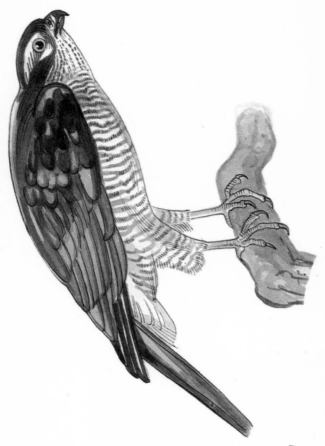

Plate 11

Plate 12

# THE BUZZARD

*Buteo buteo*

---

**EGGS:** Two to four, bluish white with light rust or brown markings, laid from April to May.

**NEST:** Branches, sticks, wool, grass, although at times an empty crow's or rook's nest is used. Located in high trees or on a cliff ledge.

**FOOD:** Mice, voles, rats, young hares and rabbits, frogs, snakes and large insects.

**HAUNTS:** Prefers wooded hills and gently sloping rocky areas.

**GENERAL NOTES:** A large bird, the Buzzard can usually be recognized by its long glides and the peculiar blunt wings. Plumage is a deep brown, although there are wide colour variations. Tail is black-and-brown barred. Another characteristic is the almost cat-like mewing cry of the Buzzard. Rabbits and small mammals form the bulk of its diet. In spite of persecution, it has maintained, and in some places increased, its numbers. As in the case of all accipiterine birds, the female is larger than the male.

Plate 12

Plate 13

# THE HOBBY

*Falco subbuteo*

---

**EGGS:** Two to four, brownish in colour, usually mottled with a deeper shade. Laid in late May or June.

**NEST:** Seldom builds its own, preferring to take over an abandoned crow's nest. Will not, however, nest away from a tree.

**FOOD:** Insects, small birds and bats.

**HAUNTS:** Wooded areas.

**GENERAL NOTES:** This is one of the smallest of the true falcons, the males measuring only a foot in length, the females from an inch and a half to two inches longer. In medieval times it was the lady's falcon. Plumage is slate-blue above, white on breast streaked with chestnut and black. There is a distinct black moustache line on the face. Although it occasionally takes small birds it must be counted as beneficial since the main part of its diet is composed of insects, caught on the wing. Moderately common in parts of Europe, the Hobby is only a summer visitor in Great Britain, seen normally between April and September.

Plate 13

Plate 14

# THE KESTREL

*Falco tinnunculus*

---

EGGS: Three to five, laid during April and May. Light brown, heavily blotched with darker brown.

NEST: Crudely constructed of sticks and twigs, although like the Hobby it will take over an empty crow's or rook's nest. Occasionally found along cliffs.

FOOD: Mice, rats, voles, moles, insects, rarely small birds.

HAUNTS: Widely distributed in rural areas, with some slight preference for wooded areas and sections characterized by cliffs.

GENERAL NOTES: The Kestrel, like the Hobby, must be counted as beneficial because of its diet. The male is as in the illustration, the female an overall red brown, with a barred tail. The Kestrel is a resident of Great Britain and our most common true falcon. In contrast to the gliding flight of most falcons, the kestrel is a hoverer. It is often mistaken for a Sparrow Hawk and blamed for the depredations of the latter.

Plate 14

Plate 15

# THE CAPERCAILLIE

*Tetrao urogallus*

---

EGGS: From six to twelve, a dull buff colour with heavy blotching of a dark red. Laid in April or May.

NEST: A hollow scratched in the ground, or in fallen foliage. Little or no lining.

FOOD: Berries, young buds and shoots, some insects.

HAUNTS: Scottish and European forests and woodlands. The Capercaillie is entirely a forest bird and is not to be found away from its haunts.

GENERAL NOTES: The largest of the grouse family, the Capercaillie became extinct here about the end of the 18th century, was reintroduced into Scotland in the 1830s and has since established itself firmly. The male is half again as large as his mate, reaching a length of three feet. The plumage in courtship is blackish with a deep iridescent sheen. The cock birds carry a distinctive red wattle over their eyes. Courtship displays occur annually, the cocks singing and strutting in competition.

Plate 15

Plate 16

# THE BLACK GROUSE

*Lyrurus tetrix*

---

**EGGS:** From seven to ten, brown mottled red or buff. Laid from April through May.

**NEST:** A hollow scratched in the ground, with a crude lining of leaves, heather or other dry vegetation.

**FOOD:** Insects, young leaves, buds and shoots, seeds, catkins and berries.

**HAUNTS:** Moorland and forest edge. Roosts in trees at night.

**GENERAL NOTES:** A spectacular bird, the Black Grouse is well known for its lyre-shaped tail and the black plumage of the cocks during winter and spring. At other seasons of the year, the male is as drab as his barred and buff spotted mate. Courtship displays are constant during the mating season, but once the cocks have selected their several mates, the hen birds brood and rear the hatch without help from the cocks. Cocks are called 'Black Cocks', hens 'Grey Hens'. The cry is a harsh cawing crow.

Plate 16

Plate 17

# THE PARTRIDGE

*Perdix perdix*

---

**EGGS:** From eight to twenty of an olive or brownish green. Laid between April and May.

**NEST:** A scratched hollow, often on ploughed ground, and lined with grass or leaves.

**FOOD:** Insects, caterpillars, grain, young shoots, grass and weed seeds.

**HAUNTS:** Usually arable land or rough pasture.

**GENERAL NOTES:** One of our more common game birds, the Partridge carries light grey plumage, barred and streaked with chestnut. The face and throat are also chestnut although there are a considerable number of colour variations. Most birds, both male and female, carry a chocolate or chestnut horseshoe marking on the breast. Seen in spring and summer months in pairs but during autumn and winter as coveys. Valuable ally to man for its insect diet, the Partridge has nevertheless suffered recently through the indiscriminate use of chemical insecticides and herbicides. Average length is twelve inches.

Plate 17

Plate 18

# THE QUAIL

*Coturnix coturnix*

---

EGGS: Six to ten, buff spotted or blotched with brown. Laid between May and June.

NEST: Grass, woven into field or hedge herbage.

FOOD: Insects, young grass or grain shoots and weed seeds.

HAUNTS: Arable and pasture land.

GENERAL NOTES: This tiny little bird is a visitor here, normally arriving in April and leaving again in late September or early October. It is considered a rarity although the population of visitors fluctuates considerably from year to year. About seven inches long, the Quail looks rather like a miniature Partridge. The overall plumage is a red-buff carrying streaks of cream and black. On the back there is considerable mottling with a dark brown. Some males carry dark stripes on the throat and neck. The Quail is a shy bird and when disturbed usually takes refuge by crouching deep in the grass so that it is seldom seen.

*Plate 18*

Plate 19

# THE PHEASANT

*Phasianus colchicus*

EGGS: Six to eighteen, a very pale olive, laid between April and June.

NEST: A hollow in the ground, usually natural and concealed by close growing vegetation or a hedgerow. The nest is lined with fine grass or leaves.

FOOD: Grain, young shoots, seeds, insects and berries.

HAUNTS: Mainly woodland although at certain times of the day the bird may be seen feeding in open areas.

GENERAL NOTES: The Pheasant is a bird introduced here from its native home in south-eastern Europe and Central Asia. Hardy and adaptable, it has established itself here as our foremost gamebird. Many of the cock birds show a wide colour variation, some almost black specimens having been seen recently. The hens, with slightly shorter tails, are quiet-looking birds with a mottled dark brown and buff plumage. The cocks call raucously, usually late in the evening or early morning.

Plate 19

Plate 20

# THE WATER RAIL

*Rallus aquaticus*

EGGS: From six to twelve, an off-white or very pale buff, with spotting of lighter brown.

NEST: A woven structure, made by both birds, of reeds and other aquatic vegetation. Located in centre of dense reed beds.

FOOD: Insects, larvae, tadpoles, fish spawn, crustaceans, some seeds and berries.

HAUNTS: Reed beds and thick marshes.

GENERAL NOTES: A highly secretive bird, more often heard than seen. The cries have a wide range, the best known being a sudden loud scream or an equally loud groan. The Water Rail is a nervous bird and hides itself in its reed-bed home at the slightest disturbance. The plumage is a chestnut brown above, well spotted and barred with black. The underside is a blue or lavender grey, shading off to a buff. The beak, which is extensively used to probe in mud, is a fairly bright red-orange.

Plate 20

Plate 21

# THE MOORHEN

*Gallinula chloropus*

---

EGGS:
From seven to twelve, a rufous buff with a heavy spotting of a deeper red. Laid between April and July. There are records of a second brood being reared.

NEST:
Built near the water's edge of reeds, grass and rushes. Lined with finer grass. May be on the ground, in low trees, or shrubs overhanging the water.

FOOD:
Aquatic life of all types — animals, insects, plants, molluscs and crustaceans.

HAUNTS:
Almost any body of inland water — lakes, meres, ponds, canals, marshes and rivers.

GENERAL NOTES:
A familiar bird of the waterside, the Moorhen looks black at a distance, actually has a blue-green breast, with a white line along the flanks. It walks clumsily, with a mincing gait and in the water may be identified by the rhythmic jerking of its head as it swims. If captured, the bird tends to defend itself viciously.

Plate 21

Plate 22

# THE COOT

*Fulica atra*

---

EGGS:        Six to twelve of a yellow-grey colour. Laid
             from April onwards.

NEST:        Large but well concealed in waterside vege-
             tation. Constructed of reeds, grasses and any
             other available material.

FOOD:        Aquatic vegetation, grain, young grasses,
             insects.

HAUNTS:      Inland waters — lakes, ponds, meres, canals,
             rivers. May, during extremely bad weather,
             be driven to coastal marshes and tidal
             estuaries.

GENERAL      The Coot resembles an oversized Moorhen.
NOTES:       Like that bird it has green legs and feet but
             in the Coot the toes carry a lobing that
             resembles webbing. The body colour is black
             on the back, slightly lighter on the underside.
             The Coot has a conspicuous white beak and
             a frontal shield on its head. When disturbed
             it flies away rapidly, moving low across the
             water, assisting itself with swift foot beats.
             The calls are varied, some harsh and screech-
             ing, others quite soft and mellow.

Plate 22

Plate 23

# THE LAPWING

*Vanellus vanellus*

---

**EGGS:** Pointed sharply at the small end, and of a heavily splotched olive green. Usually four, laid between March and June. Nests are often robbed as the eggs are considered a delicacy.

**NEST:** A bare hollow in the ground, located almost anywhere.

**FOOD:** Almost all injurious insects and their larvae.

**HAUNTS:** Moorlands, tidal mud-flats and beaches, fields and pastures.

**GENERAL NOTES:** The long, sweeping crest of the Lapwing is a distinctive mark. Seen on the ground it is beautiful with a glossy, iridescent back. In flight, it appears to be in sharply contrasting black-and-white. It is also called the Green Plover or Peewit, from its characteristic 'peewit' cry. Counted among our most useful birds because of its wholesale destruction of harmful insects, particularly wireworms and leather jackets. The Lapwing has a heavily rounded wing and its flight, which shows a definite flapping, marks it from our other common birds.

Plate 23

Plate 24

# THE CURLEW

*Numenius arquata*

EGGS: Three or four greenish-yellow, brown blotched. Pear-shaped and laid between April and May.

NEST: Dried grass and other vegetation roughly scratched together and concealed between clumps of grass.

FOOD: Sea shore life. — shellfish, worms, small crabs and tide-pool fish as well as berries and insects inland.

HAUNTS: Tidal mud-flats, sand beaches and inland moors used as nesting grounds.

GENERAL NOTES: The cry of the Curlew is well known, a sad, not-unmusical sound of 'curlwee', of which the ' . . . wee' is heard most often. The cry is heard both by day and night as the Curlew is a night flyer. The brownish plumage is barred and patterned, the bill long and curved for mud and sand probing. On the Continent the Curlew is a migrant, moving north in spring and then flying south in early autumn. Here it is a year-round resident.

Plate 24

Plate 25

# THE WOODCOCK

*Scolopax rusticola*

EGGS: Four to six, off-white in colour, with light brown blotching.

NEST: A mere depression in the ground, normally in damp woodland. Only occasionally are a few leaves used as nesting material.

FOOD: Principally worms and subterranean insects.

HAUNTS: Damp woodlands, along ditches and overgrown canal courses.

GENERAL NOTES: A bird of moderate size, the Woodcock is widely respected by shooters as a game-bird. Its plumage is a blend of browns barred and dabbled with chestnut and black. The bill, which is long, is remarkable for its sensitivity, and serves the bird to probe beneath the ground for its food. The flight of the Woodcock is both fast and erratic, and is characterized by unpredictable zigzags. Another peculiarity of the bird is the high whirring noise set up by the wings in flight. It is from the sport of woodcock shooting that we derive our modern cocker of 'cocking spaniels'.

Plate 25

Plate 26

# THE WOOD PIGEON

*Columba palumbus*

---

EGGS:

Two, flat white in colour. Laid from April to August, in many instances a second brood hatched by early nesters.

NEST:

Built of sticks and twigs, rough in construction and flat. Usually well-concealed in thick tree and shrub foliage.

FOOD:

Anything green as well as nuts, berries and some insects.

HAUNTS:

Almost universally distributed, but especially in arable land.

GENERAL NOTES:

The largest of our resident pigeons, the Wood Pigeon is considered a pest by farmers. It is distinguishable by its white neck mark and the overall slate-grey plumage shading to pink on the neck. The neck tends to iridescence and in flight a white barring is noticeable on the wings. Our large resident population is augmented during the winter months by huge flocks of migrants arriving from the Continent. Efforts are currently being made to control their depredations on farm crops.

Plate 26

Plate 27

# THE STOCK DOVE

*Columba oenas*

---

EGGS:       Two, of a cream colour, shading to white. Laid from March to October. Often two broods a year.

NEST:       A hole in a tree, by preference, although they will use the old nest of another bird through necessity.

FOOD:       Grain, young grasses and cereals, some nuts and acorns.

HAUNTS:     Open areas, largely in the north, with woodland adjacent.

GENERAL     About three inches shorter than the Wood-
NOTES:      Pigeon, the Stock Dove reaches an average length of thirteen inches. It can be distinguished from its larger cousins by the fact that it has no white on either its neck or wings. It has a slate-grey overall colour, head and neck iridescent and a paler breast. The legs and feet are a flesh pink, while the bill is yellow shading into red at its base. Although it is a resident, the Stock Dove appears to be decreasing in numbers.

Plate 27

Plate 28

# THE COLLARED TURTLE DOVE

*Streptopelia decaocto*

---

**EGGS:** Two, laid in either May or June. White or cream in colour.

**NEST:** A woven nest, commonly in trees. Made rather carelessly of twigs and small branches, flat in outline.

**FOOD:** Insects, grain, young shoots of grass and grain, weed seeds.

**HAUNTS:** Primarily a bird of the open country it is reputedly becoming a town bird, has been observed feeding with farmyard fowl.

**GENERAL NOTES:** This bird has extended its range enormously during the last ten to fifteen years, spreading north-westward through Europe and now breeding in Britain in some numbers. Like its somewhat similar cousin the Turtle Dove, which is a summer visitor here, it is dainty, with red legs, light brown plumage marked with black and characterized by a soft purring coo-note. The collared species is distinguished from the ordinary Turtle Dove by the presence of a black half moon on the back of its neck which gives rise to the name.

Plate 28

Plate 29

# THE BARN OWL

*Tyto alba*

---

EGGS:
From four to six, of a dull white. Laying may commence in April, continuing intermittently so that a brood contains young of widely varying ages. On the Continent it is recorded that two broods are raised annually.

NEST:
None. Eggs are laid on a flat, bare spot in the owl's favourite area — a barn ledge, church spire, hollow tree.

FOOD:
Mice, moles, voles, rats, young birds, occasionally fish.

GENERAL NOTES:
Nocturnal like all the owl clan, the Barn spends its days in semi-darkness, emerges to hunt at dusk. The back plumage is sandy to brown with blue-grey spotting, the front a white with brown-grey specking. The face is peculiarly heart-shaped. Calls consist of a variety of snores and hissing screeches. The legs and feet are covered with dense, furlike soft white feathers. Valuable as man's allies since they help to keep the rodent population in control.

Plate 29

Plate 30

# THE TAWNY OWL

*Strix aluco*

---

**EGGS:** From three to four, white. Lays intermittently, beginning in April.

**NEST:** Holes in trees, possibly in deserted crow, rook or pigeon's nest. Usually no material used.

**FOOD:** Young birds, small game, rats, mice, voles, rabbits (when available), possibly fish.

**HAUNTS:** Almost any heavily wooded area.

**GENERAL NOTES:** This is the familiar owl, whose quavering 'ho . . . hoo . . . hoooo . . .' is the hallmark of the family. Slightly larger than the Barn Owl, the Tawny or Wood Owl has a rich brown plumage, barred and checked with darker bars and streaks. Within the breed there is a considerable colour variation, some specimens recorded as a dull grey. Sometimes known as the Wood Owl, this fifteen-inch species is primarily a bird of the countryside and an eager hunter. It is capable of taking quite large birds and accounts for a number of wood pigeons, in addition to song birds. The Tawny is, however, considered a valuable bird because of its assistance in rodent control.

Plate 30

*Plate 31*

# THE LITTLE OWL

*Athene noctua*

---

**EGGS:** Three to six, white in colour. Laid in April or May.

**NEST:** In a tree hollow, a hole in a stone wall, rarely in deserted buildings. Little or no nesting material is used.

**FOOD:** Small rodents, birds, insects.

**HAUNTS:** Widely distributed, although the Little Owl prefers wooded areas. It has been found occasionally in city areas.

**GENERAL NOTES:** A common bird on the Continent, the Little Owl was introduced into Great Britain around the end of the nineteenth century and quickly adapted itself to its new habitat. One of the smallest temperate owls, it measures nine inches long on average, but despite its size, it is fierce and will attack birds even larger than itself. It has a brownish grey plumage, marked and spotted with white. It snores and has a variety of cries including a 'queee-eeet' and a 'keeeewaaaak'.

*Plate 31*

Plate 32

# THE EAGLE OWL

*Bubo bubo*

---

**EGGS:** Two to four, dull white. Laid April to May.

**NEST:** On a rocky ledge or shelf, occasionally in an abandoned crow's or rook's nest. Has been known to nest in a hole in the ground. Little or no nesting material used.

**FOOD:** Rabbits, hares, ptarmigan, grouse, partridge, small rodents, frogs, snakes and fish. Has attacked young fawns.

**HAUNTS:** Dense woodlands and forest areas.

**GENERAL NOTES:** The largest of the European owls, the Eagle Owl occurs from central Asia westward, is seen only rarely in the British Isles. Specimens have been reported as far apart as Denmark and North Africa. When disturbed by man it will lower its wings and rush hissing, to the attack. The strong beak is black, the eyes a bright orange colour. The legs and feet are thickly feathered and the overall plumage a blending of various brown shades. A big Eagle Owl may reach a length of twenty-eight inches but the wing span is comparatively short.

Plate 32

Plate 33

# THE LONG-EARED OWL

*Asio otus*

---

EGGS:
Three to six, of a dead white. Laid from March to May. On the Continent two broods may be reared in a season.

NEST:
Commonly lays in old nests of crows or other large birds, but occasionally on the ground.

FOOD:
Mice, rats, moles, voles and similar small rodents, small birds and some insects.

HAUNTS:
Forests and woodlands, with a marked preference for areas with a high percentage of conifers.

GENERAL NOTES:
A moderately rare bird, the Long-Eared Owl is known for its peculiar barking cry, broken by 'yaps'. The 'ears' which are really tufts of feathers are quite long and of a brown hue, blending with the overall buff plumage. The basic colour is marked on the underparts with brown streaking while the back carries both grey and brown spotting. Before its evening flight the Long-Eared Owl indulges in a bout of beak-snapping and wing beating.

Plate 33

Plate 34

# THE CUCKOO

*Cuculus canorus*

EGGS: Exact number laid is unknown, most authorities agreeing that the clutch may range as high as twelve. The eggs vary in colour, often match those of the foster-parents.

NEST: The Cuckoo builds no nest of its own, parasitizes other birds by laying in their nests. Almost any other bird may be used as host-parent.

FOOD: Caterpillars and other insects.

HAUNTS: Almost universal in its distribution.

GENERAL NOTES: Reaching a length of slightly over a foot, the Cuckoo is widely known as the harbinger of spring. Its characteristic 'cuckoo' call is heard almost everywhere, once the spring migration begins. Adult birds are slate blue-grey above, white underneath the dark grey barring. In the immature birds the back, neck and head are brown. Although the Cuckoo renders man a service through its diet, the habit of nest parasitization causes the death of countless fledglings from the host bird families.

Plate 34

Plate 35

# THE NIGHTJAR

*Caprimulgus europaeus*

EGGS: Two, white with brown or grey blotching. The eggs are peculiarly elongated.

NEST: Little or none. No nesting materials are used, the eggs often laid on bare ground or in a roughly scratched hollow.

FOOD: Insects. Most food is taken on the wing so that the main prey are moths and beetles.

HAUNTS: Peculiar to heathland and adjacent open woodlands.

GENERAL NOTES: A medium sized bird, the Nightjar seldom exceeds a length of eleven inches, and is more often seen than heard. Its plumage of grey, barred and striped with buff, black and chestnut gives ideal camouflage against the background of its habitat. A summer visitor, the Nightjar winters in South Africa, has a cry like that of a sewing machine in action. Also called the Goatsucker, it has a short, wide gaping beak, fringed with stiff, short bristles. Dormant during the daytime, the Nightjar flies with a swooping bat-like motion in search of its food at dusk and shortly after.

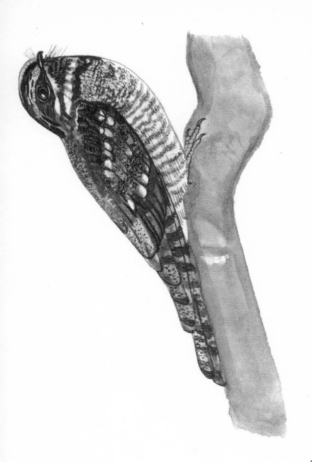

Plate 35

Plate 36

# THE SWIFT

*Apus apus*

---

EGGS: Two to four, elongated and white. Laid in May and June.

NEST: A complex structure of grass, straw, feathers and odd rubbish. This mass of material is concreted together by saliva from the Swift and is built into a nest under eaves, in attics, barn, lofts or attached to a tree. The nest is in the form of a shallow cup.

FOOD: Insects of any sort, caught entirely on the wing.

HAUNTS: Universally distributed, Swifts have been seen in the largest cities as well as the open countryside.

GENERAL NOTES: A graceful, fast flying little bird, the Swift is possibly best known for its screaming cry of 'kee-ree-ree' usually heard from high in the sky. Plumage is a dark brown verging on black, with one lighter, nearly white, spot on the chin. The Swift is a summer bird here, spends its winters in central and southern Africa.

Plate 36

Plate 37

# THE ROLLER

*Coracias garrulus*

---

EGGS: Four to five, off-white. Laid June or early July.

NEST: In a hollow tree, deep and protected. Little nesting material is used. The numbers of this bird are rapidly decreasing due to a lack of nesting places. Both birds take turns incubating.

FOOD: Insects, lizards, young mice and voles.

HAUNTS: Prefers deciduous woodlands.

GENERAL NOTES: A beautifully coloured migrant, the Roller winters in Africa, comes north to Europe during the warmer summer months but has only rarely been observed here. The plumage shows a brown back, with blue wing coverts, a greenish-blue head, blue undersurface and the tail and wings purplish but decorated with a band of silvery cobalt. Shy by nature, the Roller is an aerial acrobat with a harsh squabbling cry of 'racker-racker-racker'. During the incubation period the male birds often indulge in display flying in the nest areas.

Plate 37

Plate 38

# THE BEE-EATER

*Merops apiaster*

---

EGGS: Five to eight, white in colour. Laid May or June.

NEST: A tunnel or burrow is dug into a river bank or on occasion in flat, sandy ground. The tunnel with a small entrance, bores inward until it opens out into a circular chamber which is the actual nest.

FOOD: Insects taken on the wing. One of the favourite foods is the bee, which makes the bird anathema to apiarists.

HAUNTS: Rural areas by preference, particularly those with suitable nesting facilities.

GENERAL NOTES: The Bee-eater is a true exotic of the European bird world, ranging as far north as Spain and south central Europe. Its brilliant colouring is indicative of its tropical origins but it is remarkably hardy, arriving in Europe about May, migrating south again toward the end of August. It winters from Africa through to Kashmir, and is reputed to rear a second brood during the winter months.

Plate 38

Plate 39

# THE KINGFISHER

*Alcedo atthis*

---

EGGS: Roundish and white in colour. Six to eight laid between April and June.

NEST: A hole or tunnel dug into a river bank. The tunnel usually runs into the bank for about three feet and ends in a chamber. Here the actual nest, of dried fish bones, is built.

FOOD: Small fish, tadpoles, water insects.

HAUNTS: Rivers, lakes, occasionally found on the coast.

GENERAL NOTES: Slightly larger than the House Sparrow, the Kingfisher is a brilliantly coloured bird, with a vivid blue top which shows a greenish iridescence on the wings and crown. The ear covert and the underparts are chestnut, while the chin and each side of the neck carries white. The flight is swift, consisting in large part of dives from an observation point into the water beneath, in search of food. The colouring, and the rapidity of flight has led many observers to compare them with living jewels. The bird is double-brooded.

Plate 39

Plate 40

# THE HOOPOE

*Upupa epops*

---

**EGGS:** Four to eight, of a light pale greenish blue. Laid in May or June.

**NEST:** Usually no nesting material is used. Located in hollow trees, ash or willow by preference.

**FOOD:** Insects and larvae, grubs, woodlice, worms.

**HAUNTS:** Woodland areas.

**GENERAL NOTES:** One of our rarer and more spectacular birds, the Hoopoe occurs throughout Europe and as far east as Japan. It winters in Africa and India, is known in Great Britain solely as a migrant. Formerly it was hunted here for its plumage and as a result no longer nests in the British Isles. Feathers are a cinnamon-brown, barred with black and white. The crest is held erect at moments of excitement, showing the black tips. It takes its name from the repeated 'hoop-hoop-hoop' cry and is a rather shy creature. The Hoopoe is becoming increasingly rare throughout its range through a lack of suitable nesting facilities.

Plate 40

Plate 41

# THE GREEN WOODPECKER

*Picus viridis*

---

EGGS:       Four to eight, white in colour. Laid in April or May.

NEST:       A hole in a tree, usually deciduous. If it is available the birds will bore into dead wood.

FOOD:       Grubs, worms and larvae of insects which infest trees, as well as ants. When insects are lacking, the Green Woodpecker will take fruit, berries and nuts.

HAUNTS:     Woodlands and forest, also occasionally seen in and around garden trees.

GENERAL     The Green Woodpecker is valuable for the
NOTES:      protection it renders our forests. It searches by creeping up a tree, tapping the bark and probing for insects and grubs with its strong bill. The cry is a laughing 'hulluw-hulluw'. Plumage is green above, greenish yellow below, with a red crowned head. There is an additional spot of red on the nape of the bird's neck. The plumage of the sexes is similar save for the moustache stripe, which is red-centred in the male, black in the female.

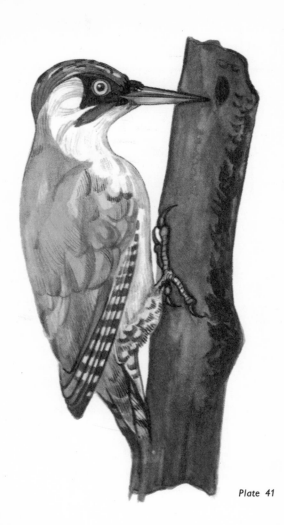

Plate 41

Plate 42

# THE GREAT SPOTTED WOODPECKER

*Dendrocopos major*

EGGS: Three to seven of a cream-white. Laid in late May or early June.

NEST: A hollow or hole in a tree. Normally dug out by the birds themselves.

FOOD: Tree-boring or damaging insects and larvae. When insect food is not available will eat berries, fruit and nuts.

HAUNTS: Woodlands and forests.

GENERAL NOTES: Plumage on this handsome bird is black and white above, with a largish red patch on the nape of the neck (this is absent in the female). The underside is cream or white shading to a bright crimson on the belly and under the tail. The young birds have a red crown, which changes to black when they reach maturity. The Great Spotted is noted for its repeated drumming on the trunks of trees, a sound which carries for some little distance. The basic cry is a sharp 'cheeck-cheeck'.

Plate 42

Plate 43

# THE BLACK WOODPECKER

*Dryocopus martius*

---

EGGS:       Three to five, white in colour and pear-
            shaped. Laid between the end of April and
            mid-May.

NEST:       In a hole in a tree.

FOOD:       Insects and larvae. Especially fond of ants.

HAUNTS:     Woodlands and forests.

GENERAL     The largest of the European woodpeckers,
NOTES:      the Black, or Great Black as it is sometimes
            called, has a length often in excess of eighteen
            inches. The jet-black plumage is broken
            only by the red cap and crest of the male,
            the occipital patch of the female. At one
            time it was considered a British visitor but
            today there seems little to substantiate such
            a view. It is a bird which clings to its home
            territory and is too strong a flyer to be blown
            away from the dense forest of its home. In
            its haunts it is a quiet bird, keeping away
            from man where possible.

Plate 43

Plate 44

# THE WRYNECK

*Jynx torquilla*

---

EGGS: From six to twelve, an off-white colour. Laid from May to July.

NEST: No nesting material is used. Uses an abandoned woodpecker hole or something similar for it seldom digs its own nest hole. Has been known to nest in a clay bank.

FOOD: Insects and their larvae, with a preference for ants.

HAUNTS: Woodlands and parks.

GENERAL NOTES: Increasingly scarce in Great Britain, the Wryneck is at best a summer visitor. The name derives from the bird's habit of cocking its head at odd, twisted angles. The plumage is brown and brown-grey above, the underparts a finely barred buff. Like its close relatives the Woodpeckers, the Wryneck has a long tongue which it projects forward to secure its insect prey, and like many of them the tongue has a sticky coating to assist in the work. Today most specimens seen in Great Britain are to be found in the southeast.

Plate 44

Plate 45

# THE SPOTTED FLYCATCHER

*Muscicapa striata*

---

EGGS: Four to six, off-white with a sprinkling of red-brown spots. Laid from May to June.

NEST: A somewhat crude structure but thickly lined. Usually hung in the concealment of thick bushes or shrubbery.

FOOD: Insects, especially those which fly.

HAUNTS: Thinly wooded areas, copses and gardens.

GENERAL NOTES: The Spotted Flycatcher is a summer visitor in Great Britain, arriving in late April through May and taking its departure in early October. It is an inconspicuous bird, its back plumage a dull brown grey, the underside a very light grey-white. Its call is high and harsh, somewhat like the scraping of metal. Most of its time is spent perching in wait for its insect prey. Motionless, it attracts but little attention. In flight, however, its speed and brilliant twisting and turning attract the eye as it unerringly swoops after its food.

Plate 45

Plate 46

# THE BLACKCAP

*Sylvia atricapilla*

---

**EGGS:** Three to five, olive or yellow white, speckled with red-brown. Laid in May in Great Britain, while on the Continent two broods are recorded.

**NEST:** Well woven, small structure of hair, dried grasses and any other suitable material. Well concealed in shrubbery, thick bushes or in low trees.

**FOOD:** Insects, larvae and berries.

**HAUNTS:** Parklands, forest edges, gardens.

**GENERAL NOTES:** A tiny songster, with an average length of five and one half inches, the Blackcap appears in Great Britain every summer. Its song is often compared with that of the nightingale, while the Germans nickname it 'the monk' for its grey robes and black skull cap. The female may be distinguished from her mate by the fact that her cap is a bright reddish-brown. Occasionally a pair of Blackcaps will over-winter in Great Britain, particularly in the southwest, where the climate permits.

Plate 46

Plate 47

# THE WHITETHROAT

*Sylvia communis*

---

EGGS:    From three to seven of an off-white with heavy speckling of red-brown. Laid from May to June.

NEST:    Well constructed in bushes, hedges or brambles, constructed neatly of roots, dried grasses, horsehair and sheep's wool.

FOOD:    Almost any type of insect, some seeds and berries.

HAUNTS:  Hedgerows and woodlands.

GENERAL NOTES:    The Whitethroat is a rather shy summer visitor, arriving in Great Britain about the end of April and leaving in early October. It is one of man's many bird allies, taking a heavy toll of the summer insect life. It has been known to raise two families in one season. The Whitethroat is readily distinguished by the grey cap and rump of the male and the white underparts of both sexes. The males are ardent, if somewhat unmusical songsters, their principal song a short and broken warble, rather harsh to the ear.

Plate 47

*Plate 48*

# THE BARRED WARBLER

*Sylvia nisoria*

---

EGGS: Four to six, off-white and blotched with grey-brown. Laid in June.

NEST: Somewhat bulky but well made, of roots, dried grasses and well lined with horsehair or fibres.

FOOD: Soft insects, some berries.

HAUNTS: Hedgerows, thickets and copses, preferably along the course of fresh-water streams.

GENERAL NOTES: The Barred Warbler is like most of the family a shy bird, avoiding man wherever possible. It arrives in Europe from its African winter home rather later than the other warblers, and only occasionally reaches Great Britain. In the adult male the upper parts are a brownish grey, the underside grey-white and distinctly marked with cross-barring. Its song is musical, a long low warbling and it is also noted for its ability to imitate the cries and calls of other birds.

Plate 48

Plate 49

# THE LESSER WHITETHROAT

*Sylvia curruca*

---

EGGS:       Four to six, off-white, grey and brown speckled. Laid in late May or early June.

NEST:       Built close to the ground and well hidden. Made of fine roots, grass and hairs, woven so as to be transparent in some cases.

FOOD:       Small insects. Some berries and soft fruit.

HAUNTS:     Woodlands, parks, hedgerows and copses.

GENERAL NOTES:    The Lesser Whitethroat is slightly smaller than its namesake and somewhat shyer. The head is a pale grey with darker markings on the ear areas. The under parts are light in colour while the upper areas are grey shading to brown on wings and tail. Arriving in April it leaves again for its winter home about mid-September. The Lesser Whitethroat has a variety of calls, its main song a rattling trill which normally begins with a soft and sweet warble. Another characteristic cry is an 'etak.tak.tak' uttered while hunting its insect prey.

Plate 49

Plate 50

# THE GARDEN WARBLER

*Sylvia borin*

---

EGGS:
Four to six, of a yellow-green, off-white, well blotched or mottled with red-brown. Laid from May through June.

NEST:
A large, loosely constructed nest, set in brambles or wild rose so as to gain protection from the thorns. Made of dried grasses, fine roots and other fibrous material.

FOOD:
Mainly insects and their larvae, some soft fruit.

HAUNTS:
Thick bushes, copses, hedgerows.

GENERAL NOTES:
An inconspicuous but pretty little bird, with an olive brown drab top which shades off to a pale buff on the underside. It arrives in the British Isles during April, usually remains until late September. The main song is a low, long warble, sweeter in tone than that of many of the other warblers. It is secretive in its habits, clinging closely to the dense undergrowth of its haunts. For this reason it is better known for its song than its actual appearance.

Plate 50

Plate 51

# THE ICTERINE WARBLER

*Hippolais icterina*

---

EGGS:      Four to six, with a brown-pink ground colour, dappled with a darker purple-brown. Laid in May to June.

NEST:      Dried grass stems interwoven with bits of bark, leaves, moss and wool. Located in small trees, well clear of the ground.

FOOD:      Insects and their larvae.

HAUNTS:      Parklands, semi-open bushes, gardens, woods and copses.

GENERAL NOTES:      One of the prettier migratory warblers, the Icterine is approximately the size of a sparrow, has olive-green upper parts, with brownish wings and tail, while the underparts are a uniform, delicate, lemon yellow. Its song and cries are varied and it is an accomplished mimic. Although normally only a rare migrating visitor in Great Britain, it has once nested here. Its summer range is the whole of Europe, south of the Baltic Sea.

Plate 51

Plate 52

# THE WOOD WARBLER

*Phylloscopus sibilatrix*

---

EGGS:
From four to six, laid in May or June. White in ground colour with heavy speckling of a dark purple-brown.

NEST:
Built on the ground, domed in shape and made of leaves, horsehair, grass, moss and wool.

FOOD:
Insects and their larvae.

HAUNTS:
Any area with trees, preferably hardwoods.

GENERAL NOTES:
A summer visitor, arriving in late April and leaving again about the end of August. The upper plumage is a light olive-green, the underside is white. The throat and both sides of the neck are yellow and above either eye is a distinct pencil stripe of yellow. The Wood Warbler has a song which has been compared with a hissing stutter, broken by trills. Occasionally the Wood Warbler uses an intermittent call note of a low tone repeated periodically. A slender bird, it is still one of the largest of our warblers.

Plate 52

Plate 53

# THE GRASSHOPPER WARBLER

*Locustella naevia*

---

EGGS:       From four to six, off-white and speckled or
            spotted with a light red-brown. Laid between
            May and July.

NEST:       Built either on the ground or close to it, in
            some convenient and well hidden spot. Made
            of dried grasses and other fibres, often con-
            cealed in a tuft of grass.

FOOD:       Insects and their larvae.

HAUNTS:     Reed beds, marshes, commons and down-
            land.

GENERAL     A summer visitor to Great Britain, seen
NOTES:      between April and September. About five
            and one half inches in length, it has a dull
            olive-brown plumage which is slightly lighter
            on the underside. It gives a somewhat mottled
            or striped appearance when first seen. The
            Grasshopper Warbler is one of the most
            secretive and inconspicuous members of the
            family. Its song is a continuous whirring noise
            which rises and falls and has been compared
            with the sound of our common grasshopper.
            At one time it was called the Green Reed
            Warbler.

Plate 53

Plate 54

# THE REED WARBLER

*Acrocephalus scirpaceus*

---

EGGS: Three to five with a green-white ground colour, olive spotted. Laid between May and July.

NEST: Carefully woven cup form, of wool, horsehair, grass and moss. Usually built suspended between the stems of several reeds or occasionally in a bush or corn stalks.

FOOD: Insects and their larvae, some berries.

HAUNTS: Reed beds, marshes and lake shores. Occurs in Great Britain most commonly in the south, has been observed as far north as Yorkshire but only rarely in Wales.

GENERAL NOTES: An inconspicuous summer visitor, with no distinguishing markings. The plumage on the upper parts is a soft dull brown, shading to a lighter colour on the underside. The song is a sustained series of two or three basic notes, with imitations introduced. The bird is one of the few species which sings at night. It leaves about mid-September and winters in eastern Africa.

Plate 54

Plate 55

# THE GREAT REED WARBLER

*Acrocephalus arundinaceus*

---

EGGS: Four to six with a bluish-green ground colour. The eggs, which are laid in May and June carry brown blotchings.

NEST: Similar in type and construction to that of the Reed Warbler. Slightly larger, it is still skilfully woven of the best available materials and is almost invariably placed somewhere in the reed beds, suspended between two stems.

FOOD: Insects and their larvae.

HAUNTS: Reed beds, marshes and meres.

GENERAL NOTES: The Great Reed Warbler is one of the largest of the entire warbler family, its size comparing with that of the starling. Like most of the warblers it is a migrant, reaching Europe in late April or early May, departing again in September. Common throughout Central Europe, it is only an occasional visitor to the British Isles, seen in the reed beds of East Anglia and along the southern coast.

Plate 55

Plate 56

# THE GOLDCREST

*Regulus regulus*

---

**EGGS:** From six to eleven, minute in size, white in ground colour. A faint speckling of red-brown occurs. Laid between April and June.

**NEST:** Made in the form of a hanging basket and woven with care from moss, grasses and occasionally spiders' webs. Often lined with feathers, the Goldcrests' nests are hung in fir trees.

**FOOD:** Insects, all of a small size, with greenfly a favourite.

**HAUNTS:** Woodlands, conifer plantations, copses and hedgerows.

**GENERAL NOTES:** Sometimes called the Golden-Crested Wren, the Goldcrest is our smallest bird and is, in fact, the smallest of all Europe. Often overlooked because of its size (three and one half inches), it is nevertheless an exquisite creature. The plumage is a soft olive-green, the beak and legs are dark and both sexes carry a crest — the female's being yellow, the male's orange. When the birds are excited the crests are raised. The song is high and trilling, could be compared to the ringing of a tiny bell.

Plate 56

Plate 57

# THE FIELDFARE

*Turdus pilaris*

---

EGGS:      Three to six, blue-green in colour. Laid April to June, in some cases two broods.

NEST:      Carefully woven out of grasses, fibres, rootlets. Lined with mud and located in trees of various sorts.

FOOD:      Insects, worms and fruit.

HAUNTS:      During the winter in open areas and fields. In the remainder of the year the Fieldfare is a bird of the forest edge, often found among fir trees.

GENERAL NOTES:      The Fieldfare is a moderate sized bird, reaching a length of ten inches. Its back plumage is brown, the wings and tail shading to a very dark, rich tone. The breast, which is a lighter brown, is dappled with blackish markings. The rump and head are grey. It is a winter visitor to the British Isles, when it may be seen mixing in the hedgerows with other members of the thrush family. In certain parts of the Continent it is considered a gamebird.

Plate 57

Plate 58

# THE SONG THRUSH

*Turdus philomelos*

---

**EGGS:** Four to six with a turquoise ground colour and black speckling. Laid between March and July, sometimes in two sittings.

**NEST:** Carefully woven of moss, grass, rootlets and other available material, smoothly lined with mud. Placed low in hedges, trees and bushes.

**FOOD:** Insects, grubs, slugs and snails. Noted for its habit of breaking snail shells on stones. Some berries and other fruit are included in its diet.

**HAUNTS:** Widespread and varied, from forest edge to town parkland.

**GENERAL NOTES:** Possibly the best-known member of the thrush family, the Song Thrush is widespread throughout the British Isles and Europe. Its top plumage is brown, while the underside is a buff white liberally spotted with dark brown on the breast. Its song is loud and clear, with a repetitive refrain sounding rather like 'Come out, come out, come out'. There is also a quiet cry, heard when the bird is food gathering, which is the simple sound 'cheek'.

Plate 58

Plate 59

# THE BLACKBIRD

*Turdus merula*

EGGS: From three to six, with a bluish-green ground colour, finely spotted with brown. Laid between March and July. There are records of three broods being hatched within one season.

NEST: Grass, horsehair, fine roots plastered together with mud and often given a finer, inner lining of grass. Placed in trees, bushes, shrubs or creepers.

FOOD: Essentially insect eaters, the Blackbirds have created quite a bit of damage where there is soft fruit.

HAUNTS: Varied and general with almost universal distribution.

GENERAL NOTES: As the name implies the male is jet-black and has an orange beak. The female is a dark brown which shades off into a blackish tone at the tail. The hen bird's beak is brown, in contrast to her mate's. Cock birds with extensive patching are not uncommon and complete albinos have been reported.

*Plate 59*

Plate 60

# THE WHEATEAR

*Oenanthe oenanthe*

---

EGGS: Three to six, pale blue-green in ground colour with faint, fine brown specking. Laid in April or May.

NEST: Crudely constructed of grass and weeds. Located under stones, clods of earth, in old rabbit holes and occasionally in the cracks of old stone walls.

FOOD: Insects, grubs and other pests. Valuable ally to man because of its diet.

HAUNTS: Open fields, moors, downlands.

GENERAL NOTES: The Wheatear arrives in Great Britain during March, leaves again for its African winter home in mid-October. Song is short and sharp, and rather cheerful. A shy bird, the Wheatear is readily marked by its white rump, the black banding on its tail and the well-marked black ear coverts. The pale grey upper parts shade off to a buff-cream on the underside. The hen bird is more buff in her overall plumage but still carries the white rump.

Plate 60

Plate 61

# THE ROBIN

*Erithacus rubecula*

EGGS: Five to eight of an off-white ground colour with minute rust-coloured speckling. Laid from February to July.

NEST: Well constructed and sometimes vaulted. Composed of grass, wool, hair, rootlets and any available fibres. Indiscriminately placed — in trees, shrubs, in empty tin cans, on shed ledges, even under tree roots.

FOOD: Insects of all sorts and their larvae, some berries, and scraps of all sorts.

HAUNTS: Widespread distribution from woodlands and forest to cities.

GENERAL NOTES: Probably our best-loved bird, friendly and intelligent. Has been known to 'adopt' a house or a family. Upper plumage is brown, breast on both sexes is red. Immature birds are brown with distinct speckling over all. The song is varied, a high clear tone with a wide range of notes broken with twittering. Calls include a scolding 'tic .. tic .. tic.' The Robin is medium sized, up to five and a half inches, appears to have large eyes and extremely slender legs.

Plate 61

Plate 62

# THE NIGHTINGALE

*Luscinia megarhynchos*

---

EGGS: Three to six of a pale olive shade, with overtones which range from blue to brown. Laid in May or June.

NEST: Made of grasses, roots and dead leaves. Located on the ground or slightly up in low bushes, shrubs or young trees.

FOOD: Insects and their larvae, occasionally berries.

HAUNTS: Copses, thickets and the edges of woodlands.

GENERAL NOTES: Widely celebrated for its song, the Nightingale is a summer visitor arriving in April and departing in late September. It is inconspicuous and shy with a dull brown plumage which lightens on the underside. Both sexes are alike in plumage and markings. The song, which is most noticeable at night, is loud, full of deep notes and with an extensive run of trills and warbles.

Plate 62

Plate 63

# THE WHITE-SPOTTED BLUETHROAT

*Luscinia svecica cyanecula*

EGGS: From four to seven. Off-white, sometimes bluish, in ground colour with some faint speckling. Laid in June.

NEST: Compact and well-woven of grasses, rootlets and hair. Concealed in reed-beds, scrub or hummocks of grass.

FOOD: Insects and their larvae, some berries.

HAUNTS: Lakeshores and river banks, among willow and reed-beds.

GENERAL NOTES: This bird is a rare spring visitor to Britain, on its way from Africa to its breeding grounds in Central Europe. The male's blue throat patch with its white centre makes it easy to distinguish, even from the Scandinavian race, the Red-Spotted Bluethroat. The latter has chestnut instead of white in the blue patch and is seen more often in autumn. The Bluethroats are rather robin-like in appearance and activity, and reach a length of about five and one half inches.

Plate 63

Plate 64

# THE WHINCHAT

*Saxicola rubetra*

---

**EGGS:** From four to six, bluish-green in ground colour, occasionally specked with a soft red-brown. Laid in May or June.

**NEST:** Woven of grass, hair, twigs and rootlets. Placed in the ground concealed in thick grass; rarely in low overhanging bushes.

**FOOD:** Insects taken on the ground or in the air.

**HAUNTS:** Commons, open country, with a preference for gorse-covered moorlands.

**GENERAL NOTES:** A summer visitor, the Whinchat arrives in mid-April, is gone again by the beginning of October. The cock bird is much more strikingly marked than the hen, with a black cheek and a distinct white line above the eye. At the base of the tail there is a white mark on either side and further barring is seen on either wing. The back is strongly barred, the breast is a soft red-brown, almost pink. The female lacks the characteristic black markings. The song is short, sung in what amount to bursts of notes.

Plate 64

Plate 65

# THE REDSTART

*Phoenicurus phoenicurus*

---

**EGGS:** Five to seven of a very pale turquoise blue. They may occasionally show a faint brown blotching. Laid in May and June.

**NEST:** Rudely constructed, with a variety of materials — grass, hair, wool, leaves, moss and feathers. Placed in a tree, in an abandoned rabbit hole, a mud-bank or even a quarry side.

**FOOD:** Insects and their larvae.

**HAUNTS:** Widespread but the Redstart prefers to haunt areas with at least a few trees.

**GENERAL NOTES:** Similar in size and habit to the Robin, the Redstart is a summer visitor. It is less common and far shyer than the Robin and is seen in Great Britain only from April through September or October. In the cock bird the forehead is white, the cheeks and throat black, the upper plumage grey. Both sexes share the bright red tail and rump, while on the cock the breast is also reddish.

*Plate 65*

Plate 66

# THE BLACK REDSTART

*Phoenicurus ochruros*

EGGS: From four to seven, white in colour. Laid in April or May. It has raised two broods in a season in some areas.

NEST: Loosely made of grass, hair, feathers, wool and leaves. Placed in holes, under eaves or inside farm buildings.

FOOD: Insects, taken on the wing in the main; at times berries and soft fruits.

HAUNTS: Widespread. Known in Great Britain largely as a summer migrant, a small colony has been observed in the Home Counties which is over-wintering.

GENERAL NOTES: A duller bird than the Redstart, the Black Redstart is characteristically grey with a rufous tail and rump. The female's plumage has a brown tinge to its grey but she too has the orange-red tail. The bird has a warning call of quick, sharp ticking sounds, while its song is rather high in tone. Like the Redstart it is a valuable friend to man due to its high insect intake.

Plate 66

Plate 67

# THE DIPPER

*Cinclus cinclus gularis*

---

EGGS:      From three to six, of a pure white colour.
           Laid from early April to June. There are
           records of two broods reared within a season.

NEST:      Built neatly and carefully in a dome shape
           with the entrance low on one side. Materials
           are usually leaves, grasses·and moss. In some
           cases a complete outer casing of green moss
           has been reported. It is placed as close as
           possible to the water, sometimes behind
           a little waterfall, within a rock crevice.

FOOD:      Small fish, aquatic insects and their larvae
           as well as snails.

HAUNTS:    The banks and edges of swift moving, clear
           fresh water.

GENERAL    Quick moving and quiet the Dipper looks like
NOTES:     an oversized Wren, with a dipping movement
           and short high-cocked tail. It pursues its
           food underwater, swimming, diving and
           walking along the bottom. Upper plumage
           is brown on the head shading to dark grey.
           Breast and throat are white, the belly dark
           brown shading to black. Another name for
           the Dipper is Water Ousel.

Plate 67

Plate 68

# THE WREN

*Troglodytes troglodytes*

---

EGGS:     From five to seven, of a pure white heavily spotted with tiny dots of red. Laid between April and June. Records show that two broods are not uncommon.

NEST:     A complex and carefully constructed dome, with a round entrance hole located at one side. Made with whatever materials are most easily available — moss, leaves, straw, hay, grass, feathers, hair. Located in or on banks, walls, bushes, hedgerows or low trees.

FOOD:     Insects, chiefly caterpillars and tree grubs.

HAUNTS:   Widely distributed, found in gardens, copses and hedgerows.

GENERAL   One of our smallest residents, the Wren is
NOTES:    known for its loud singing and for its angry 'churrring' to warn trespassers near its nest. One of the peculiarities of the bird is the fact that more than one nest is built. Seemingly the hen makes her choice and the 'spares' are used as roosting spots in bad weather. More than forty wrens have been counted in such a spare.

Plate 68

Plate 69

# THE RED-BACKED SHRIKE

*Lanius collurio*

---

**EGGS:** Four to seven of varying colours. Most are grey-buff, others may be greenish. Large ends are often blotched. Laid in May or June.

**NEST:** Twigs, fine grasses, moss, wool and hair, Built in bushes or hedgerows.

**FOOD:** Large insects, small birds, mice and frogs.

**HAUNTS:** Thorn thickets, hedgerows, telephone wires.

**GENERAL NOTES:** Known also as the 'Butcher Bird', the Red-Backed Shrike is a summer visitor to Great Britain, arriving toward the end of April and leaving again in the beginning of October. In the cock bird the head and rump are grey, the back chestnut. There are sharp black ear coverts and the underside is a reddish buff. The tail, which is black, carries white marking on either side. The hen bird is reddish brown above with a light cream underside. The cry of the Shrike is sharp and harsh, a rasping, 'check .. check .. check'.

Plate 69

Plate 70

# THE WOODCHAT SHRIKE

*Lanius senator*

---

EGGS:    Five to seven, with an olive-green ground colour. Many are spotted or blotched with patches of grey or browns. Laid in May and June.

NEST:    Well made nest, concealed in thick foliage. Made of grasses, leaves, hair, and bits of wool.

FOOD:    Small birds, large insects, frogs, lizards.

HAUNTS:    Forest edges and large open orchard-like areas.

GENERAL NOTES:    A rather brightly coloured European summer migrant, the Woodchat Shrike is seldom seen in Great Britain and is becoming increasingly rare in much of its Continental range. The cock bird has the crown of its head and the lower part of its neck in a bright chestnut, the forehead and ear coverts are black, the wings are black and white and the rump is pure white. Like many of the Shrike family the Woodchat impales its prey on thorns before flaying and eating it.

Plate 70

Plate 71

# THE WAXWING

*Bombycilla garrulus*

---

EGGS:       Four to seven with a pale blue ground colour, purplish markings lying under the shell and black splotching on the shell. Laid in June and July.

NEST:       Loosely built of twigs, small roots and moss. Placed, normally, about ten feet from the ground in small trees.

FOOD:       During summer months the Waxwing is largely an insect eater but during the winter it is a berry eater.

HAUNTS:     Forest areas and open woodlands.

GENERAL     An occasional winter visitor in Great Britain,
NOTES:      the Waxwing is one of the most exotically coloured northern birds. About the size of a Starling it carries a chestnut crest and has a broad black stripe running through and above the eye from the bill. The tail is grey at its base, turns black toward the tip and terminates in a broad band of bright yellow. Each wing carries a white-and-scarlet bar, the scarlet made up of a substance like sealing wax at the tip of each feather.

Plate 71

Plate 72

# THE GREAT TIT

*Parus major*

---

EGGS: From six to twelve with a ground colour of white and delicately placed red spots. Laid in April and May.

NEST: Grasses, moss, feathers, wool or any other available material. Located almost anywhere — tree holes, eaves, stone walls, flowerpots.

FOOD: Scraps and fat, nuts, seeds and insects.

HAUNTS: Extremely wide distribution.

GENERAL NOTES: The largest of the tits, the Great Tit is a resident of Great Britain and a handsome bird with an average length of five and one half inches. It carries yellow, green and blue plumage, has a black-and-white head and may be distinguished from its close relatives by the black stripe which runs on the underside from chin to tail. It is not a musical bird but has a series of calls the most notable of which sound like the Spanish 'Si . . . si . . . si'. The song sounds like the word 'Tee-cher . . . . . tee-cher . . .'

Plate 72

Plate 73

# THE BLUE TIT

*Parus caeruleus*

---

EGGS: Seven to thirteen, white ground colour, dotted with a rufous-tan. Laid in April or May.

NEST: Constructed of any readily available material, and placed without apparent regard to any rule. Main ingredients in building are hair, feathers, wool, moss, leaves and very fine grass. May be built in almost any location although tree holes are sought by preference.

FOOD: Natural diet is of insects but has come to depend on scraps and fat provided for it.

HAUNTS: Almost universally distributed in Great Britain.

GENERAL NOTES: Sometimes called the Tom Tit, the Blue Tit is an accomplished feathered acrobat. They are often observed hanging upside down, hunting for food, or more simply disporting themselves. An adaptable bird, the Blue Tit lives in perfect harmony with man, accepts nest-boxes and food without a qualm. Smaller than the Great Tit, it also lacks the distinguishing line from chin to tail.

Plate 73

Plate 74

# THE COAL TIT

*Parus ater*

---

EGGS: From five to eleven. Basic colour is white with light red spotting, similar to that of the Blue Tit. Laid between April and late May.

NEST: Fine grasses, moss wool, hair, man-made fibres. Cleverly concealed in a stump, hole, or occasionally on the ground.

FOOD: Insects and their larvae, particularly those which attack trees. Also nuts and seeds.

HAUNTS: Almost universally distributed in Great Britain but especially fond of gardens and open wooded sections.

GENERAL NOTES: Slightly more sombre in colouring than the other resident tits. Cap and throat are black, while both sexes carry a white spot on the nape of the neck which easily distinguishes them from other tits. In general plumage the upper parts are a deep olive-brown, while the underparts shade to a buff. Like all the tits, the Coal is an acrobat but it has a peculiar song, described as 'Ifhee . . . ifhee . . ifhee'.

Plate 74

Plate 75

# THE CRESTED TIT

*Parus cristatus*

---

EGGS:   From five to six, white in ground colour and carrying rust-red spots. Laid end of April or early May.

NEST:   Usually built in a tree trunk but when such a site is not available the Crested Tit will take over an abandoned crow or magpie nest. In any case it is lined with moss, hair, grasses and bits of wool.

FOOD:   Insects, their eggs and larvae.

HAUNTS:   Wooded areas, occasionally seen in parklands during the winter months.

GENERAL NOTES:   In Britain, the Crested Tit is restricted to the Scottish Highlands. It is, however, widely distributed on the Continent. It is about the same size as the Coal Tit and has an appearance of chubbiness. Its colour is dull brown above, shading to buff on the undersides. The crest is white plentifully marked with black. The cheeks are white and there is a distinctive black bib. Like all tits the Crested is gregarious and flocks of them may be seen together during the winter months.

Plate 75

Plate 76

# THE MARSH TIT

*Parus palustris*

EGGS: From six to nine, with possibly a second brood of an equal size. The eggs are white with red-brown spotting and are laid from end of April into May.

NEST: Located in tree holes, sometimes found on the ground. Made of many materials, depending in large part on their availability — usually wool, moss, grass and hair.

FOOD: Insects and their larvae as well as seeds.

HAUNTS: Woodlands, orchards, gardens, copses and marshes.

GENERAL NOTES: Similar in coloration to the Coal Tit, the Marsh Tit lacks the white on the nape of the neck and its underside is lighter in tone. Again it differs from the Coal Tit in that it has no wing bar. Somewhat shyer than the other members of its family, it is most often seen in winter when flocks of Marsh Tits gather to hunt seeds.

Plate 76

*Plate 77*

# THE LONG-TAILED TIT

*Aegithalos caudatus*

---

EGGS:
From six to sixteen with a white ground colour plentifully speckled with rust-red spots. Laid in April and May. Second broods have been recorded.

NEST:
Complex, domed structure with the entrance hole located close to the top at one side. Built of moss, wool, fur, hair, feathers, and other available material, it is thoroughly felted and given a feather lining. Concealed by foliage, usually in the fork of a tree branch.

FOOD:
Insects and their larvae as well as seeds.

HAUNTS:
Hedgerows, woodlands, thickets and copses.

GENERAL NOTES:
Distinguishable from the other members of the tit family by its long tail, the Long-Tailed Tit carries black and white plumage, the white being shaded with pink. During the time that the hen is incubating and rearing the young, both parents sleep within the nest. A rare sub-species exists in which the head is all white; it is, however, more common in Europe, and occurs here only occasionally.

Plate 77

Plate 78

# THE PENDULINE TIT

*Remiz pendulinis*

---

EGGS:

Five to seven, off-white in colour. Laid in May or June.

NEST:

A pendulant structure, hung from tree branches or sometimes from reeds. It is constructed of tightly woven grasses and weeds, and has a funnel type of entrance on its upper surface.

FOOD:

Insects and seeds.

HAUNTS:

River banks and lake shores.

GENERAL NOTES:

The Penduline Tit is common in southern Europe and seldom if ever moves north into temperate climates. It derives its name from the hanging nest, which is characteristic of this type of tit. Approximately the size of a wren, it is primarily a bird of the reed beds, in which it finds both food and sanctuary. In appearance it is typically a tit, and its quick darting movements also show its close relationship to the types we know here.

Plate 78

Plate 79

# THE SWALLOW

*Hirundo rustica*

---

EGGS:
From three to six, with a white ground colour. They are somewhat long and carry a plentiful speckling of brown. Laid between May and August, with two broods quite usual.

NEST:
Mud, feathers, straw and grass, plastered together in the form of a shallow, open cup. Usually plastered on a ledge or wall, rarely in trees.

FOOD:
Insects, taken on the wing.

HAUNTS:
Widespread.

GENERAL NOTES:
The Swallow is one of our best known migrants, arriving in Great Britain about the first of April, leaving again at the end of October. The back and wings have a distinctive blue sheen and the throat is a dark chestnut, banded with blue. Most of the Swallow's life is spent on the wing and its feet and legs are consequently quite weak. Its arrival here is usually a sign that spring has come and in some places the annual migration is almost clocklike in its precision.

Plate 79

Plate 80

# THE HOUSE MARTIN

*Delichon urbica*

---

EGGS:
From four to six, long and tapered in shape, white in colour and laid between June and August.

NEST:
Built of similar materials to those used by the swallows — mud, straw and grass — it differs in shape. The House Martin nest resembles a closed cup, with a side entrance located near the top. It is placed under eaves or in similar locations. Two broods are quite usual.

FOOD:
Insects, normally caught on the wing.

HAUNTS:
Widespread. Very often around farm buildings.

GENERAL NOTES:
Black plumage and a distinct white rump are the marks of the House Martin, another summer visitor. It has a shorter, broader tail than the Swallow, is more gregarious, large flocks perching together. The feet are covered with soft, down-like feathers.

Plate 80

Plate 81

# THE SAND MARTIN

*Riparia riparia*

---

EGGS: Three to five, elongated in shape and white in colour. Laid from May through July.

NEST: Loosely constructed of hay, straw and feathers. Located in a small chamber at the end of a tunnel, which may be from a foot to eighteen inches in length. These tunnels are burrowed out in sand-pits, clay-banks or cliff sides. The Sand Martin is a colonial nester, several hundred nests often located in one bank. Usually double-brooded.

FOOD: Insects, taken on the wing.

HAUNTS: River banks and other areas which offer nesting sites.

GENERAL NOTES: Slightly smaller than the House Martin, the Sand Martin lacks the white rump of its cousin, and has a brown band across its white chest. The back and wings are a dark brown. Like all the swallow family it is a migrant, arriving in Great Britain about March and leaving toward the end of September.

Plate 81

Plate 82

# THE NUTHATCH

*Sitta europaea*

EGGS: From four to ten, ground colour white and carrying heavy spotting in a brownish red. Laid from April to June.

NEST: Located in a hole, usually in a tree trunk. Lined with grass and leaves. If the entrance is too large, the Nuthatch will stop it up with mud to suit.

FOOD: Insects and their larvae; seeds and berries, hazel nuts, etc.

HAUNTS: Any area with a good supply of trees.

GENERAL NOTES: The Nuthatch can often be spotted as it walks up or down the trunk of a tree, diligently searching for insects. Its back and wings are a soft blue, the underparts a buff which shades to chestnut on the belly. It has a startlingly clear whistle which sounds like 'tuuy . . . tuuy' as well as a sharply metallic trill. Its habit of partially filling its nest entrance has earned it the nickname of 'Mudstopper' in some European countries.

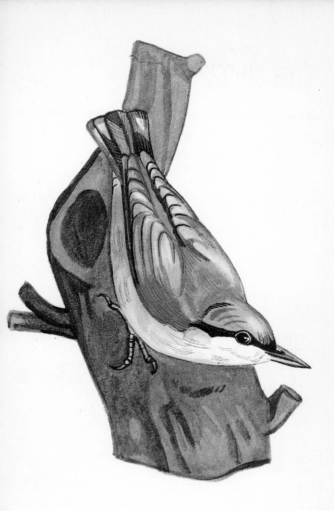

Plate 82

Plate 83

# THE SHORT-TOED TREE CREEPER

*Certhia brachydactyla*

---

**EGGS:** Five to seven with a white ground colour, heavily spotted with brown. Laid in May and June. Double broods are quite common.

**NEST:** Holes in trees, cracks in walls or even under loose bark. Made of grass, bark, hair, bits of wool and moss.

**FOOD:** Insects and their larvae, particularly those which live in and on trees.

**HAUNTS:** Woodlands, forest, parks and gardens.

**GENERAL NOTES:** The Short-Toed Tree Creeper is properly a European bird, but it is much like our own resident Tree Creeper. The essential difference is in the relative length of the back-toe claws. Both birds are insect eaters who spend much of their lives searching the trunks of trees for food. The hunt is always from the ground up, never from the top down, and is accomplished with a peculiar jerking movement. The Short-Toed Tree Creeper is, however, a shy and inconspicuous bird whose brown mottled plumage forms an almost ideal camouflage.

Plate 83

Plate 84

# THE HAWFINCH

*Coccothraustes coccothraustes*

EGGS: From three to six, off-white with streaks and blotchings of brown. Laid in April and May.

NEST: Grasses, roots, hair. Located high in a tree or bush.

FOOD: Seeds, nuts, buds, berries, insects and larvae.

HAUNTS: Widespread but localized distribution usually in orchard or garden areas.

GENERAL NOTES: One of the larger finches, the Hawfinch reaches a length of seven inches and is a thickset bird. It has an immensely powerful beak which it uses to crack open fruit stones in order to eat the inner pith. Apart from the nesting season, the Hawfinch tends to roam, covering large sections of the countryside. One of the easiest means of identification is through the white band at the tip of the tail feathers which is unmistakable in flight.

Plate 84

*Plate 85*

# THE GREENFINCH

*Chloris chloris*

---

EGGS:      From four to six, laid between April and July. Many instances of double broods have been recorded. The eggs are a buff-cream, heavily streaked and spotted with a purplish-black and rust-red.

NEST:      Well made of grasses, roots, straw, hair and moss, with a feather lining. Placed in bushes or hedges.

FOOD:      Weed seeds and some insects.

HAUNTS:      Widespread, distributed over almost all country areas.

GENERAL NOTES:      Not quite as large as the Hawfinch, the Greenfinch is an inconspicuous bird, its soft green plumage blending easily into the countryside foliage. The yellow of the wings and tail is almost lost when the bird is not flying. In the winter months the overall green of the plumage becomes even duller as the individual feathers develop brown tips. The Greenfinch is noted for its twittering song which has earned it the name, in some areas, of Green Linnet.

Plate 85

Plate 86

# THE GOLDFINCH

*Carduelis carduelis*

---

**EGGS:** From four to six, laid in May and June. Off-white with brown and purple-black spotting.

**NEST:** A small, well-built structure, located usually in low trees or bushes, often in and around orchards. Made from grasses, moss, wool, hair, fine leaves and tiny roots.

**FOOD:** Weed seeds and insects.

**HAUNTS:** Widespread but tends to seek areas with heavy weed growth — wasteland and pastures.

**GENERAL NOTES:** Probably the most handsome of our native finches the Goldfinch is almost exotic in appearance with its vivid and intense colouring. The combination of red, golden-yellow, black and white make it an unmistakable species. Even its song is odd: a tinkling twitter, often compared to the sound of little bells. It was formerly much in demand as a cage bird although now, like all of our wild birds, it is protected by law. Its voracious appetite serves man well since it consumes a vast quantity of weed seeds which would otherwise germinate.

Plate 86

*Plate 87*

# THE SISKIN

*Carduelis spinus*

---

EGGS:   Four to six, laid between April and June. Where seasons and climate permit there are double broods. Eggs are off-white with a blue-green shade, dappled with light brown.

NEST:   Located in trees, conifers where possible. Well made of moss, lichen, grass, hair, wool and fibre.

FOOD:   Insects and larvae as well as weed seeds.

HAUNTS:   Conifer forests, chiefly in Scotland and the north.

GENERAL NOTES:   Formerly a favourite cage-bird, the Siskin was kept for its restless activity and its song rather than its plumage. It is a small bird, usually reaching a length of four and a half inches, with dull brownish-green back plumage which shades into yellow on the rump. The breast, which is yellow-green, shades off to a white on the rump. The cock birds have black crowns and some also carry a blackish chin. The hens are not as brightly coloured as their mates. Many Siskins arrive here during the winter but a certain number are resident, largely in Scotland.

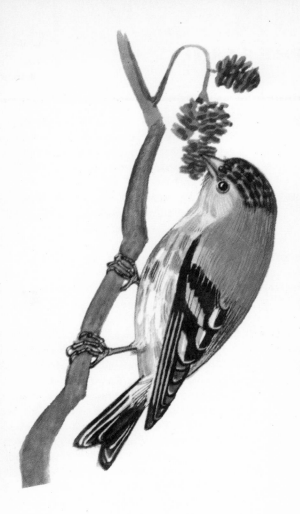

Plate 87

Plate 88

# THE LINNET

*Carduelis cannabina*

---

EGGS: Three to six of a very pale blue-green, speckled with rust-brown. Laid between April and June, with many cases of double broods recorded.

NEST: Placed in hedgerows or bushes the Linnet nest is neat and well-made. It is usually built of fine grass, hair, fibre, rootlets and wool.

FOOD: Insects and their larvae, weed seeds.

HAUNTS: Widespread distribution but most often found in weed-grown wasteland or on open heaths.

GENERAL NOTES: The Linnet is world famous as a singer and has often been compared to the Canary but in actual fact most Linnets have a wider range and show a more definite musical personality. The male birds lose their red forehead and breast during the winter months, becoming a rather drab grey-brown, which more nearly matches the duller hens. After the nesting season Linnets tend to form small flocks, roaming the countryside in search of food.

Plate 88

Plate 89

# THE REDPOLL

*Acanthis flammea*

---

EGGS: From four to seven, pale blue-green, spotted with light brown. Laid between May and June.

NEST: Made from rootlets, grass, hair and moss, the nest is well concealed in trees, hedges or bushes.

FOOD: Insects and their larvae, weed seeds.

HAUNTS: Primarily a tree-loving bird, the Redpoll may be encountered wherever trees are found but is more frequently seen in the north.

GENERAL NOTES: Similar in many ways to both the Siskin and the Linnet, the Redpoll is a pretty little bird. On average four and one half inches in length, the cock birds carry a crimson forehead, rose tinted breast and a black chin. The basic plumage is a soft, striped brown. The hen birds lack the rose on the breast and both sexes lose some of their colour during the winter. At that time the overall colour tone is one of grey. The song of the Redpoll is not particularly remarkable but they are noted for continuous activity, which is usually accompanied by a constant twittering sound.

Plate 89

Plate 90

# THE SERIN

*Serinus serinus*

---

EGGS: Four to five, off-white, blotched with dark reddish brown. Laid in May or June.

NEST: Neat, compactly woven from grass and straw, lined with horsehair and feathers. Placed in low trees or bushes.

FOOD: Weed seeds mainly.

HAUNTS: Widespread distribution, typically found in gardens, woodlands and parks.

GENERAL NOTES: Not normally found in Great Britain the Serin sometimes reaches here by accident, carried by storms. It is a handsome little bird, closely related to the Canary and like it, a songster, although the Serin has neither the range nor the ability of its cousin. It has, however, a considerable reputation as a flyer, some authorities comparing its flight ability to that of the Martins. The Serins normally spend their summers in central Europe, winter in southern Europe or North Africa.

Plate 90

Plate 91

# THE BULLFINCH

*Pyrrhula pyrrhula*

---

**EGGS:** Three to six, laid between April and June. The eggs are a deep blue-green and heavily spotted with brown and black. Double broods are quite common.

**NEST:** Placed in a low tree or bush, the nest is made largely of twigs and roots and moss or lichen.

**FOOD:** Buds, seeds and insects.

**HAUNTS:** Widespread distribution, with considerable local variation.

**GENERAL NOTES:** The black head, grey-blue back and red breast of the cock Bullfinch are unmistakable. His mate is more sombre, lacking the colourful breast but both show a white rump. Although they are handsome birds they tend to be terrifically destructive in and around orchards. Much of their diet is composed of buds and a small flock of Bullfinches can play havoc with fruit trees. In some sections their raids have been so heavy that they have been removed from the protected list, at least temporarily.

Plate 91

Plate 92

# THE CROSSBILL

*Loxia curvirostra*

---

EGGS:
Three or four, laid very early in the year, from February onward. Off-white with a green tint and marked with rust-brown spots.

NEST:
Tightly and firmly woven of pine twigs, grass and hair, moss and lichen. Usually placed in a fir or other conifer, well protected.

FOOD:
Seeds from fir cones, as well as other seeds.

HAUNTS:
Woodlands, either mixed or coniferous. Occurs most commonly in the north.

GENERAL NOTES:
The Crossbill is readily distinguished by the fact that the tips of the two halves of its bill cross. The adult cock bird is red overall with brown wings and tail, while the hen is a dull olive-green, striped and marked with brown and yellow. Immature birds are marked like their parents but have orange and yellow shadings. The Crossbill is not common here but there is a small resident population in Scotland and East Anglia, often augmented by winter visitors who arrive from Scandinavia.

Plate 92

Plate 93

# THE CHAFFINCH

*Fringilla coelebs*

---

EGGS: From four to six, laid in April and May. Ground colour is usually an off-white tinged with pink, with blotchings of dark brown.

NEST: Round and well made, found usually in a bush or low tree, often in the fork of a branch. Made of hair, moss, roots, fine grass and feathers. In some cases an outside camouflage covering is added.

FOOD: Weed seeds, berries and insects.

HAUNTS: Extremely widespread. The Chaffinch makes its home in almost any area, with the exception of city centres.

GENERAL NOTES: One of our more common birds, the Chaffinch has adapted itself to life with humans to a remarkable degree, only the Sparrow exceeding it in this ability. The cock birds have bright pink breasts, and their back plumage is brown changing to olive on the rump, while the crown is a slate blue. The hens are slightly smaller and a bit duller in colouring. Both sexes have white barring on the wings. One noticeable call of the Chaffinch is its repeated cry of 'Pink . . . Pink . . .'

Plate 93

Plate 94

# THE YELLOWHAMMER

*Emberiza citrinella*

---

EGGS: From three to six, laid in May or June. They are off-white in ground colour and marked with curling hair-like lines of a dark purple.

NEST: Rather crude, made of grass, moss and wool or hair. Set on the ground or rather low in the hedgerows and bushes.

FOOD: Weed seeds, berries, soft fruit and insects.

HAUNTS: Widely distributed in open country, most common in hedgerows.

GENERAL NOTES: The Yellowhammer is one of our more common birds. About six and a half inches long it has a variable plumage, the older birds showing a brighter, richer yellow. The young cocks are nearly all brown, only the head showing the characteristic yellow. The hen birds are similarly marked, but duller and with more striping on the background tones. The song is a monotonously repeated note, at the end the final note being just a fraction higher. The Yellowhammer is known all over Europe.

Plate 94

Plate 95

# THE CORN BUNTING

*Emberiza calandra*

---

EGGS:
From three to six, laid in May and June. Off-white ground colour, sometimes with a slight reddish tint. Markings are dark brown or yellow-grey.

NEST:
Loosely constructed of grass, leaves, straw, twigs, hair and wool. Usually placed on the ground but well concealed and protected.

FOOD:
Insects and their larvae as well as grain and weed seeds.

HAUNTS:
Widespread distribution, inhabiting thickets, hedgerows and downlands.

GENERAL NOTES:
The Corn Bunting is our largest representative of the family, reaching a length of about seven inches. It is a quietly coloured bird, resembling the Sky Lark in many ways. The plumage is a dull brown above with darker streaks, the underside a buff, the breast and flanks marked with a blackish-brown. Some Corn Buntings turn an overall buff colour or cream and there have been records of bright yellow specimens. The song is somewhat brittle, a harsh tinkling sound often preceded by a series of almost mechanical clickings.

Plate 95

Plate 96

# THE HOUSE SPARROW

*Passer domesticus*

---

**EGGS:** From four to six, laid at any time between February and October. Ground colour is a darker shade. Multiple broods are the rule rather than the exception.

**NEST:** An untidy heap of straw, grass and feathers, built in any convenient nook, crevice or cranny.

**FOOD:** Grain, insects, scraps, seeds.

**HAUNTS:** Almost universally distributed here. The House Sparrow is as common in urban centres as on farms.

**GENERAL NOTES:** One of our commonest, and probably our most prolific bird. Just under six inches long, the cocks are distinguished by their black bibs and dark grey caps, the hens being a drab brown. The cheeks are white in the cock, which enables the watcher to tell it from the Tree Sparrow. The cries and calls consist mainly of a series of chirps, uttered for varying periods. The cocks are peculiarly aggressive during the mating seasons. The bird was introduced in the New World, just over one hundred years ago. It is now considered a pest in the United States.

Plate 96

Plate 97

# THE TREE SPARROW

*Passer montanus*

---

**EGGS:** Three to six, laid between April and June, often in double broods. Light brown in colour with darker speckling.

**NEST:** Similar in form to the House Sparrow, an untidy mass of straw, grass and feathers. Placed in holes, crevices or occasionally in hedgerows, usually in a colony.

**FOOD:** Insects, grain and weed seeds.

**HAUNTS:** Woodlands, copses and thickets. In harsh weather it may venture closer to man and his dwellings.

**GENERAL NOTES:** Slightly smaller than the House Sparrow, the Tree Sparrow is shyer, avoiding man where possible. On the cock birds the cap is a bright brown and the black bib is much smaller. The white of the cheek is broken by an irregular black patch. Both sexes are marked alike. The Tree Sparrow has a song rather like that of its city cousin but it is higher in tone, a succession of quick chirps sometimes broken by churring.

Plate 97

Plate 98

# THE CRESTED LARK

*Galerida cristata*

---

EGGS: Three to five, grey-white in colour with abundant speckling in either dark or light brown. They are laid from April to June with double brooding common.

NEST: Loose and simply built, dried grass, straw, weeds, sometimes lined with horsehair. Placed on the ground beneath tussocks of grass, in ditches or any other hiding place.

FOOD: Insects, grain and weed seeds.

HAUNTS: Fields, meadows, roadsides, during the winter in towns and villages.

GENERAL NOTES: A fairly common bird on the Continent, the Crested Lark occurs in Great Britain only accidentally. It is distinguished from the other members of its family by the crest of about a dozen feathers which spring directly from the scalp. The song is a melodious whistle and the Crested Lark is often kept as a cage bird not only for its own song but also for its ability to imitate the calls and cries of other birds.

Plate 98

Plate 99

# THE SKY LARK

*Alauda arvensis*

---

EGGS: Three to six, laid between April and June, with double-brooding usual. The ground colour is off-white and there is a dense speckling of various shades of brown.

NEST: A hollow or depression in the ground, in pasture or possibly grain fields. There is little attempt at concealment which is unfortunate since lark eggs are eagerly sought by many of our corvines.

FOOD: Sprouting grain and grass, insects and weed seed.

HAUNTS: Open country — moors, downs, heaths and meadows.

GENERAL NOTES: At one time this lovely little songster was so plentiful that it was netted on the Sussex Downs for shipment to the London poultry markets. It is today protected and is often the harbinger of spring. The sweet song is usually heard while the bird is on the wing, spiralling upward. The Sky Lark is an inconspicuous bird, its plumage a dull brown striped with a darker shade. The outer tail feathers carry white, identifiable in flight. There is a small crest which lies close to the head save when the bird is excited.

Plate 99

Plate 100

# THE TREE PIPIT

*Anthus trivialis*

---

**EGGS:** Four to seven laid during May and June. There is a wide variation in the colour, the most commonly found being dull white so heavy blotched with brown as to seem completely brown.

**NEST:** Well hidden and on the ground. Concealed usually by overhanging branches or thick brambles although occasionally found hidden only by grass. Made of dried grasses and lined with wool, hair or down.

**FOOD:** Insects and their larvae, weed seed, some grain.

**HAUNTS:** The edges of woodlands or semi-open country with a goodly number of trees.

**GENERAL NOTES:** The Tree Pipit is a summer visitor in Great Britain, arriving in April and leaving in late September or early October. In appearance it is much like our resident Meadow Pipit, from which it differs largely in habitat. It averages six inches in length and carries light brown upper plumage, shading to buff on the underside with brown bars both top and bottom. Its movements along the ground are quick, typical of the wagtail family. Musical trilling song, often given in descending flight from a tree or other song post.

Plate 100

Plate 101

# THE WHITE WAGTAIL

*Motacilla alba alba*

---

EGGS:
From four to seven with a blue-white ground colour, thickly marked with grey spots. Laid in May here, on the Continent three broods are not uncommon.

NEST:
Usually in a hole — clay bank, wall, tree stump. Made of grass, hair, moss and wool.

FOOD:
Insects, normally flying types.

HAUNTS:
Frequently along water courses — lakes, rivers, canals.

GENERAL NOTES:
The White Wagtail is a rather rare summer visitor in Great Britain and when seen is often mistaken for its cousin, the Pied Wagtail. It differs, however, in having a grey back, as opposed to the black back of the Pied during the spring and summer months. It is, however, very difficult to tell the females of the two types apart, since both are grey on the back but the hen White Wagtail has less black on her crown. The movement of the White Wagtail is typical of the family, short darting rushes in a zigzag course, accompanied by up and down waggings of the tail at each halt.

Plate 101

*Plate 102*

# THE BLUE-HEADED WAGTAIL

*Motacilla flava flava*

EGGS: Five or six, white in colour with heavy dappling of grey-brown. Laid between May and June.

NEST: Well constructed of roots, moss, wool, fibres and lined with hair. Located on the ground but concealed, or in a hole.

FOOD: Small flying insects, especially flies.

HAUNTS: Open fields, marshy areas.

GENERAL NOTES: The Blue-Headed Wagtail is a rather rare bird in Great Britain, although it has been known to breed here. Its habits, haunts and appearance are much like that of our more common Yellow Wagtail. In the Blue-Headed, however, the head is a slate blue instead of the olive and yellow of the Yellow. There is, in addition, a broad white band above the eye which is absent in the Yellow. In other respects it is almost identical and the females resemble one another even more closely. It is a typical wagtail, helping to keep flies under control, and moving with the characteristic series of jerky dashes.

Plate 102

Plate 103

# THE STARLING

*Sturnus vulgaris*

---

EGGS: Four to seven of a very pale blue. Laid from April to June.

NEST: Crudely and loosely made of straw, grass, leaves and any available fibrous material. Located in holes, cracks, crevices; barns, outhouses, trees and bushes.

FOOD: Insects and their larvae, as well as large quantities of soft fruit.

HAUNTS: Almost universally distributed in Great Britain. Breeds in town and country. Large numbers roost communally in London and other large towns.

GENERAL NOTES: A moderately large bird, with a length of over eight inches, the Starling has, along with the House Sparrow, learned to live with man. There are few spots where the glossily iridescent plumage of the Starling is not commonplace. Although it aids man, in that it attacks grubs and is particularly fond of wireworms, the Starling is not an unmixed blessing. It is fond of all sorts of soft fruit, creating havoc in beds and plantations. Although it is a resident here the normal population is periodically increased by large flocks arriving from Europe.

Plate 103

Plate 104

# THE GOLDEN ORIOLE

*Oriolus oriolus*

---

EGGS: Three to five of a buff tinted white with heavy speckling of brown at the blunt end. Laid in May or June.

NEST: Well woven and placed high, in the fork of a branch, occasionally suspended between two branches. Fine grass, straw, twigs, rootlets, hair and moss.

FOOD: Insects and their larvae, as well as soft fruit.

HAUNTS: An infrequent visitor, it appears most often in the south and east of Great Britain. Habitually haunts heavily wooded areas.

GENERAL NOTES: One of our most beautiful visitors, the Golden Oriole winters in Africa and has all the brilliance usually associated with tropical birds. The body plumage is a bright yellow, the wings are black as is the centre of the tail. The beak is red and a line of black runs from the base of the beak to the eye. The hen birds are brown and buff streaked on the underside, carry a green tint on the back and head. The song consists of a series of linked musical triplets.

Plate 104

Plate 105

# THE ROOK

*Corvus frugilegus*

---

**EGGS:** Three to six, laid in March or April. Green ground colour with brown spotting.

**NEST:** An untidy collection of sticks and straw, located high. Often lined with grass and mud daubed. The Rook is a colonial nester.

**FOOD:** Insects and larvae but in addition sown grain and the eggs of song and game birds.

**HAUNTS:** Fields and woodlands.

**GENERAL NOTES:** The most common of our corvines, the Rook is noted for its raucous cawing, jet black plumage and the ragged appearance of its wings in flight. Rooks are social creatures, spending much of their lives in flocks. It is resident in Great Britain and reaches a length of about eighteen inches. Although it consumes large quantities of insect pests such as wire worms and leather jackets, it is injurious to newly planted grain fields and has a bad reputation for its depredations among the eggs of smaller birds.

Plate 105

Plate 106

# THE HOODED CROW

*Corvus cornix*

---

EGGS:  From three to six of a pale greenish blue colour, spotted thickly with brown. Laid in late March and April.

NEST:  Crude and loose, made largely of twigs, moss, heather, etc. Found on cliff ledges, tree tops, on the ground but always singly as the Hooded Crow is not a colonial nester.

FOOD:  Like most corvines the Hooded Crow is omnivorous, taking insects and their larvae, shellfish, carrion, table scraps, mice, song birds, grain and eggs of other birds.

HAUNTS:  Found chiefly in Scotland and Ireland where it is a resident, it occurs in England in winter, in many coastal areas.

GENERAL NOTES:  A large bird, with a length of about eighteen inches, the Hooded Crow's plumage is unmistakable. The head, throat, wings and tail are jet black, while the remainder is an ashen-grey. Its habits and reputation are similar to those of the Carrion Crow, which it replaces in many parts of its range. The Hooded Crow is, like all the members of its family, a highly intelligent bird.

Plate 106

Plate 107

# THE JACKDAW

*Corvus monedula*

---

**EGGS:** From four to seven, blue-white with brown speckling. Laid in April.

**NEST:** Made from sticks and straw, lined with fine grass, wool, moss, hair. Located in trees, in old buildings or in unused chimney-pots. Jackdaws often nest colonially.

**FOOD:** Although mainly insectivorous, they may also eat young birds, mice, frogs, grain and a certain amount of fruit.

**HAUNTS:** General with no special locations favoured.

**GENERAL NOTES:** One of our smaller corvines, the Jackdaw may reach a length of fourteen inches; it can be distinguished by its smaller size from the Rooks with which it sometimes nests. The back of its head and its neck are grey, in contrast to the black body plumage. Taken early from the nest, young Jackdaws tame readily and have learned to speak — indistinctly and in a harsh voice. Like the Magpie it seems attracted by bright objects and will often steal them, to be hidden in the nest or some other hideaway.

Plate 107

Plate 108

# THE MAGPIE

*Pica pica*

EGGS: From four to seven, of a light green-blue, brown dappled and laid during April.

NEST: A large, domed structure, composed of sticks, twigs, roots and straw plastered with mud. The entrance hole is located at one side in the top half. It is placed in a tree or sometimes a thick bush.

FOOD: Fruit, grain, nuts, insects and larvae, snails, slugs, eggs and nestlings, mice, moles and voles, occasionally leverets.

HAUNTS: Widespread, but with a preference for clumps of thorn in which refuge may be sought.

GENERAL NOTES: The Magpie's plumage is black and white, with the black showing a very high gloss. The tail is rather long and beats distinctively in flight. The voice is harsh and grating but the Magpie may be taught to speak in captivity. Like its cousin the Jackdaw, the Magpie is a thief, attracted to anything bright, be it a tin lid or a diamond brooch. Despite its somewhat showy beauty farmers and gamekeepers list it as a pest.

Plate 108

Plate 109

# THE JAY

*Garrulus glandarius*

---

EGGS:      From four to seven, laid in April or May. Usually a very pale shade of green with minute spots of rust brown.

NEST:      Rather crudely built and made of sticks, twigs, straw and roots. Located in the deepest possible cover in a low tree or thick bush.

FOOD:      Omnivorous — small mammals, small birds, insects, fruit, snails, acorns, eggs.

HAUNTS:    Woodlands and their immediate environs.

GENERAL NOTES:    The Jay is perhaps the least known member of the crow family here, with the exception of the Chough. The Jay measures about thirteen inches, carries rather colourful plumage and avoids man with fantastic skill. The overall colour is a brownish pink, the head and wings carrying black and white markings. The wings are also decorated with 'flashes' of blue, which in turn is finely lined with black and white. Since the Jay is most often seen flying away in the distance it may at times be identified by its startlingly white rump.

Plate 109

# INDEX